Ageing and Health

GW00685019

Must ageing populations create conflict between generations and crisis for health systems? Our answer is no. The problem is not so much demographic change as the political and policy challenge of creating fair, sustainable and effective policies for people of all ages. This book, based on a large European Observatory study, uses new evidence to challenge some of the myths surrounding ageing and its effects on economies and health systems. Divisive and alarmist views of population ageing are often based on stereotypes and anecdotes unsupported by evidence. How we address ageing societies is a choice. Societies can choose policies that benefit people of all ages, promoting equity both within and between generations, and political coalitions can be built to support such policies.

This title is available as Open Access on Cambridge Core.

SCOTT L. GREER is Professor of Health Management and Policy, Global Public Health and Political Science at the University of Michigan and Senior Expert Advisor on Health Governance for the European Observatory on Health Systems and Policies.

JULIA LYNCH is Professor of Political Science at the University of Pennsylvania.

AARON REEVES is Associate Professor in the Department of Social Policy and Intervention, University of Oxford.

MICHELLE FALKENBACH is Postdoctoral Associate in the Master of Public Health Program at Cornell University.

JANE GINGRICH is Professor of Comparative Political Economy in the Department of Politics and International Relations, University of Oxford, and a fellow of the Canadian Institute for Advanced Research Innovation, equity, and the future of prosperity program.

JONATHAN CYLUS is Coordinator of the London Hubs, European Observatory on Health Systems and Policies, London School of Economics and the London School of Hygiene and Tropical Medicine.

CLARE BAMBRA is Professor of Public Health in the Population Health Sciences Institute, Newcastle University.

European Observatory on Health Systems and Policies

The volumes in this series focus on topical issues around the transformation of health systems in Europe, a process being driven by a changing environment, increasing pressures and evolving needs.

Drawing on available evidence, existing experience and conceptual thinking, these studies aim to provide both practical and policy-relevant information and lessons on how to implement change to make health systems more equitable, effective and efficient. They are designed to promote and support evidence-informed policy-making in the health sector and will be a valuable resource for all those involved in developing, assessing or analysing health systems and policies.

In addition to policy-makers, stakeholders and researchers in the field of health policy, key audiences outside the health sector will also find this series invaluable for understanding the complex choices and challenges that health systems face today.

List of Titles

Challenges to Tackling Antimicrobial Resistance: Economic and Policy Responses
Edited by Michael Anderson, Michele Cecchini, Elias Mossialos

Achieving Person-Centred Health Systems: Evidence, Strategies and Challenges
Edited by Ellen Nolte, Sherry Merkur, Anders Anell

The Changing Role of the Hospital in European Health Systems
Edited by Martin McKee, Sherry Merkur, Nigel Edwards, Ellen Nolte

Private Health Insurance: History, Politics and Performance
Edited by Sarah Thomson, Anna Sagan, Elias Mossialos

Series Editors

Ageing and Health

The Politics of Better Policies

SCOTT L. GREER
University of Michigan, Ann Arbor

JULIA LYNCH
University of Pennsylvania

AARON REEVES
University of Oxford

MICHELLE FALKENBACH
Cornell University

JANE GINGRICH
University of Oxford

JONATHAN CYLUS
European Observatory on Health Systems and Policies

CLARE BAMBRA
Newcastle University

CAMBRIDGE
UNIVERSITY PRESS

CAMBRIDGE
UNIVERSITY PRESS

University Printing House, Cambridge CB2 8BS, United Kingdom

One Liberty Plaza, 20th Floor, New York, NY 10006, USA

477 Williamstown Road, Port Melbourne, VIC 3207, Australia

314–321, 3rd Floor, Plot 3, Splendor Forum, Jasola District Centre,
New Delhi – 110025, India

103 Penang Road, #05–06/07, Visioncrest Commercial, Singapore 238467

Cambridge University Press is part of the University of Cambridge.

It furthers the University's mission by disseminating knowledge in the pursuit of education,
learning, and research at the highest international levels of excellence.

www.cambridge.org
Information on this title: www.cambridge.org/9781108972871
DOI: 10.1017/9781108973236

First published 2021

Printed in the United Kingdom by TJ Books Limited, Padstow Cornwall

A catalogue record for this publication is available from the British Library.

Library of Congress Cataloging-in-Publication Data
Names: Greer, Scott L., author.
Title: Ageing and health : the politics of better policies / Scott L. Greer, University of
  Michigan, Ann Arbor, [and six others].
Description: New York, NY : Cambridge University Press, 2021. | Series: European
  observatory on health systems and policies | Includes bibliographical references and index.
Identifiers: LCCN 2021012173 (print) | LCCN 2021012174 (ebook) | ISBN
  9781108972871 (paperback) | ISBN 9781108973236 (ebook)
Subjects: LCSH: Older people – Medical care – Europe. | Older people – Medical care –
  Europe – Political aspects. | Older people – Medical care – Europe – Economic aspects. |
  BISAC: POLITICAL SCIENCE / Public Policy / Economic Policy | POLITICAL SCIENCE /
  Public Policy / Economic Policy
Classification: LCC RA564.8 .G74 2021 (print) | LCC RA564.8 (ebook) | DDC
  362.1084/6–dc23
LC record available at https://lccn.loc.gov/2021012173
LC ebook record available at https://lccn.loc.gov/2021012174

ISBN 978-1-108-97287-1 Paperback

European Observatory on Health Systems and Policies

The European Observatory on Health Systems and Policies supports and promotes evidence-based health policy-making through comprehensive and rigorous analysis of health systems in Europe. It brings together a wide range of policy-makers, academics and practitioners to analyse trends in health reform, drawing on experience from across Europe to illuminate policy issues.

The European Observatory on Health Systems and Policies is a partnership hosted by the World Health Organization Regional Office for Europe, which includes the Governments of Austria, Belgium, Finland, Ireland, Norway, Slovenia, Spain, Sweden, Switzerland, the United Kingdom, and the Veneto Region of Italy; the European Commission; the World Bank; UNCAM (French National Union of Health Insurance Funds); the Health Foundation; the London School of Economics and Political Science; and the London School of Hygiene & Tropical Medicine. The Observatory has a secretariat in Brussels and it has hubs in London (at LSE and LSHTM) and at the Berlin University of Technology.

Contents

Figures

Tables

Boxes

Acknowledgements

The authors would like to thank many people for helpful comments on previous drafts including Anna Dixon, Jonathan Hopkin, Lorelei Jones, Lucie Kalousova, Deborah Mabbett, Minakshi Raj, Holly Holder, Mauricio Avendano, Raphael Wittenberg, participants in panels at the European Public Health Association Conferences in Ljubljana and Marseille and a workshop at the University of Wales Bangor.

1 | Introduction

Life in an ageing society is a truly novel experience. For most of our species' history, a large majority of people were young and life much beyond 60 seemingly a rarity (Thane, 2005). Now, populations around the world are ageing. It might be happening in countries at different speeds and to varying extents, but it is an almost universal phenomenon. In 2000 the median age in Western Europe was 37.7; in 2020 the median age was 42.5. By 2050 it will rise to 47.1 (UN Department of Economic and Social Affairs, 2020). Looking at specific Western European countries, this trend becomes even more impressive. In Italy the median age in 2000 was 40.3, in 2020 it was 47.3 and by 2050 it will be 53.6. Spain follows a similar pattern, with a median age of 37.6 in 2000, 44.9 in 2020 and a projection of 53.2 for 2050 (Statsita, 2020). Figure 1.1 shows us by how much the population is expected to age, looking at over 65 year olds in 2010 and 2050 as a share of the total population and comparing that with over 85 year olds in 2010 and 2050.

The fact that societies are ageing is a good news story. If the twentieth century were a movie, this would be a balmy last scene, with the protagonists ageing in health and peace after a very difficult adventure. It is a story of increased wealth, better health and improved human welfare around the world.

Ageing of the population occurs for a number of reasons. People are by and large living longer than ever before. The average European born in 1950 could expect to live for 62 years based on the death rates at that time. Since then, the life expectancy of subsequent cohorts has mostly trended upwards. A European born in 2019 could expect to live for 78.6 years (Roser et al., 2019). These increases in longevity have occurred because health conditions that in previous years were a death sentence are no longer so threatening. Infant and child mortality rates, in particular, have fallen dramatically. This matters because a large part of average low life expectancies is due to childhood infectious diseases; life expectancy at age 1 has generally been higher than life expectancy

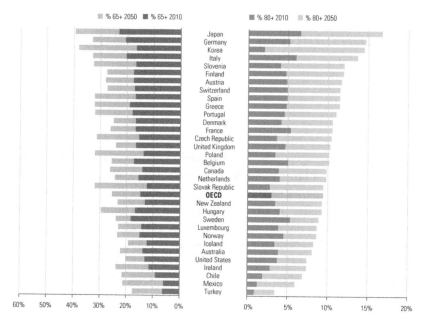

Figure 1.1 The shares of the population aged over 65 and 80 years in the OECD will increase significantly by 2050

Source: Colombo et al., 2011

at birth. The fact that life expectancy at birth in the WHO European region was 77.1 years and life expectancy at 1 was a marginally higher 77.3 years in 2015 is a sign of massive success in prenatal, perinatal and child health. Adults also have higher survival rates. To put this in perspective, consider that instead of dying at age 65 from an acute myocardial infarction thirty years ago, the same person today might survive the age 65 heart attack and eventually die of heart failure at 85.

On top of reduced mortality, fertility rates have also declined substantially, so that the average woman in 2020 was having 1.62 children, compared to 2.66 children in 1950 (UN Department of Economic and Social Affairs, 2020). Greater legal, economic and social equality for women, hard-fought policy and legal changes that increase women's reproductive autonomy, technological advances in birth control and changing expectations of life-courses all combined to reduce both desired and real fertility almost everywhere in the world. Much of the rich world has fertility below the replacement rate, presaging population decline and sparking worries.

The end result is an increase in survival and a decline in repla
These two processes are leading to a slowly increasing populatic
at older ages. While children up to the age of 17 comprise 19 per ce..
of the population in 2020 and are expected to make up 17.5 per cent
of the population in 2050, the share of the total population in Western
Europe over age 65 will increase from 19 per cent in 2020 to 28 per
cent in 2050. For those above 85 years, their share of the population
will increase from 2.5 per cent in 2020 to 5.6 per cent in 2050 (UN
Department of Economic and Social Affairs, 2020). Figure 1.2 shows
this in graphic form. For most of human history, populations looked
like Niger: a pyramid. Rich societies began to develop an urn shape
after, roughly, World War Two, with a big bulge in the middle (the Baby
Boom generation), more older people and fewer children.[1]

Some countries' populations are expected to shrink in the coming
years, if they are not already in the process of shrinking; for example,
Belarus, Bulgaria, China (and Taiwan, China), Croatia, Cuba, Czechia,
Estonia, Germany, Greece, Italy, Japan, Latvia, Lithuania, Poland,
Romania, the Russian Federation, Slovakia, Slovenia, South Korea,
Spain, Sri Lanka and Thailand. While in some cases, notably in Central
and Eastern Europe, outmigration is part of the problem, it is not the
only reason and nevertheless leaves behind demographic structures that
are unusual in world history.

At face value one would think that the fact that populations are
ageing should be celebrated. It reflects a range of successes in health
care, from reproductive health to geriatric health, but also successes in
social policy more broadly. People are living longer and enjoying all
the life experiences that come with that.

For some, though, these developments point to worry rather than
celebration. Many writers view population ageing as a threat to societies,
governments and economies. They see rising health care, long-term care
and pension costs. They see a large older population retiring *en masse*,
depriving labour markets of productive workers and leaving governments with fewer revenues generated through taxation. And they see
too few young people to compensate for these declines. In their darker

---

[1] Throughout this book, the terms 'older adults' or 'older persons' will be used
to refer to persons above the age of 65 unless otherwise specified. The reason
these terms were chosen as opposed to 'elderly' or 'senior' is because they
acknowledge the relativity of ageing (Taylor, 2011) as the ageing experience can
vary and does so from person to person.

Figure 1.2 Bell curve comparison

Source: populationpyramid.net, 2019

versions, they see entire societies becoming decadent and dying, and perhaps perishing in geopolitical competition as a result. They posit a win-lose scenario for politics and policy, in which one generation's gain is another one's loss.

These fears need not come true. They are, rather, 'zombie ideas', policy or political ideas which persist in debates despite multiple empirical refutations (Quiggin, 2010). As the rest of this introductory chapter argues, there is extensive research arguing that population ageing need not be a threat to the sustainability of states or their health care systems. As Chapters 2 and 3 show, there is not even much evidence that people who share an age share much else. Nor need there be a tradeoff between the interests of people of different ages. Rather, what we refer to throughout this book as 'win-win' solutions are possible. These are policies which do not create a political divide between people of different ages or generations, but rather those which invest over the life-course in order to maximize people's health and wellbeing. The question that matters, and which the rest of the book explores, is why win-win policies are, or are not, adopted.

1.1 Two Very Different Narratives Depicting Ageing Societies

There are effectively two simple and in fact oversimplified narratives about older people in today's society. The first is that older people are a forgotten and neglected group. They are pushed out of formal employment because of views that younger people are more productive. For reasons that largely have to do with the design (or lack thereof) of social welfare systems, they are overwhelmingly poor, lack good access to health care and live in low-quality housing. Perhaps the lack of public support afforded to them is due to concerns that expanding the welfare state would be untenable and unsustainable. And so, older people are left to suffer. This has been historically common. Societies with low poverty among older people are essentially a creation of the postwar welfare state, and they are not the norm (still rarer are the ones, notably the United States, where the elderly are less likely to be indigent than the working-age population). In Europe we can see a version of this forgotten-elderly model in Central and Eastern Europe, where healthy-looking fiscal balances can rest partly on very limited old-age security. Some societies effectively counterbalance poverty among older people with inter-family transfers (e.g. a parent who lives with adult children and might give or receive unpaid care), but reliance on strong and generous families in modern European societies is not obviously sustainable and is clearly not an adequate basis for policy in many of them.

It is also easy to find examples of ageism and age-related discrimination even in countries where public policies ensure an adequate material standard of living for older people. Care homes for older people were, for example, common COVID-19 hotspots, with terrible consequences in many places. Policies for transitions in and out of COVID-19 lockdown often blithely told 'vulnerable individuals' to stay home while reopening businesses and institutions – a sign that policymakers often failed to understand not just transmission mechanisms but also the important role older people play as employees, customers and unpaid workers in areas such as child care. A few politicians, such as the Lieutenant Governor of Texas (the state's most powerful executive position) even went so far as to say explicitly that older people should be sacrificed[2] for the greater good. Outside such stark reminders of the value that societies often place on older people's lives, the evidence for age discrimination in areas from built environment to employment decisions is impressive (Center for Ageing Better, 2020; Chang et al., 2020).

The second narrative, which is much better represented in international policy debates and the politics of some countries such as the UK and US, is that older people are primarily an entitled group. They are mostly Baby Boomers (those born just after World War Two) and as such have experienced substantial economic growth over their lifetime. They have good, steady, well-paying jobs even while youth unemployment skyrockets. They own property and other assets at a time in history when asset prices have reached historic highs. But their children or grandchildren's generations are not, or should expect not to be, nearly as prosperous as them. A recent report published by the Resolution Foundation (Bangham et al., 2019) about the UK argued that it can no longer be taken for granted that every generation will do better than the last. This is neither a surprising nor an ubiquitous trend, though; policies that lead to increasing income and wealth inequality over time should be expected to have a different effect over cohorts, with people

---

[2] 'As a senior citizen, are you willing to take a chance on your survival in exchange for keeping the America that all America loves for your children and grandchildren?' Patrick said. 'And if that's the exchange, I'm all in' (Sonmez, 2020).

who lived under more egalitarian
tages relative to the people who:
increasing inequality. In other wc
in more egalitarian times than M
effects of inequality more acutely

It is easy to find the second :
contributions to the endless over:
older people's consumption prefe
sophisticated analyses of social
writer in the *Independent* claim
society, including war, disease a:
human population outranks ther
this extraordinary claim was that
growth, labour markets, taxation, the transfer of property, health, family
composition, housing and migration will be impacted by the 'demographic agequake'. A 2016 *Time* article (Buchholz, 2016) presented
two big threats that an ageing population poses. The first is that the
number of workers supporting retirees will significantly decrease. In
the 1950s there were fifteen workers for every one retiree, while today
there are about two workers for every one retiree. The second threat,
particularly looking at the United States, is the need for more workers.
Hospital employees and restaurant waiters are positions that need to
be filled and are often done so by immigrants. The author argues that
immigrants can fragment a country's culture unless strong cultural and
civic institutions are in place, suggesting that American traditions like
hot dog cook-outs and Memorial Day parades could disappear. A 2019
piece (Pettinger, 2019) highlights the effects of an ageing population.
The dependency ratio will increase, the government will spend more
on health care and pensions, those people working will have to pay
higher taxes, there will not be enough workers to cover all the work
that needs to be done, the economy will change with more companies
focusing on retirees as clients and increased pension savings could reduce
capital investment. Rather than go on with examples from the pundit
class, it might be more entertaining to look at witty tweets that make
the same arguments.

These are all examples of the 'greedy geezer', image a phrase that a
British journalist coined for the United States (dropping the adjective
'old' that would normally accompany 'geezer' but retaining all of the
insult). Its policy theory is that older adults have it too good and that

overall, lose out as a result. Its political theory is
vote for politicians who help them to hold on to their
serve only those public sector entitlements and regula-
ensions, early retirement ages and good access to health
disproportionately benefit them, while raising taxes and debt
tting expenditures on other age groups. Even if their intentions
good, older voters and the older politicians they elect just might not
understand what younger people face, want or need (a point for which
there is evidence from Japan (McClean, 2019).

Most readers might have been nodding along with one or both of
these narratives. World literature abounds in stories of lonely and poor
older people, for the good reason that old-age security is a relatively new
and far from universal phenomenon. Punditry, and for that matter serious
policy debate, frequently invokes the opposite stereotypes – of healthy
pensioners enjoying a poolside drink in Mallorca financed by a generous
welfare state that their children will never see. Some of us, including the
authors in this project, had also nodded along at such stories, laughed
at quips about gerontocracy or 'OK boomer', and drawn implications
from the pronounced correlations between age and partisan votes. But
research, including that of the European Observatory on Health Systems
and Policies' Economics of Healthy and Active Ageing series (of which
this book is a part), showed us just how faulty, and pernicious, those
stories are (to summarize the book very simply: Chapters 3 and 4 show
how faulty they are; Chapters 5 and 6, how pernicious).

To understand the politics of ageing and health, and to get to win-win
policies, requires recognition of not just how flawed these narratives
are but how little power age has as an explanatory category in politics.
This book is a work of interdisciplinary social science, but one about a
topic where everybody has some experience and can understand, from
multiple angles, the different decisions people make. Those decisions
are diverse: whether it is parents who work to give their children a nice
inheritance, children who leave work to care for parents, grandparents
whose caring work permits their children to work, or just parents who
do their best to introduce their child to people who might give them a
good job. Generations and cohorts are made up of people with different
ideas, assets and strategies. That fact, rather than stylized ideas about
how entire generations behave, is the right starting point and one that
gives us a sense of what age can explain about the treatment of older
people in health, and its limitations as an explanation.

1.2 What Are the Consequences of Seeing Popula
in a Negative Light?

Perhaps above all else, the catastrophist narrative of pe
provides someone to blame for other people's proble
labour fallacy, which says (incorrectly) that there is a fixeu a...
jobs, resonates with younger people struggling with high youth unemployment. As of January 2020, *before the COVID-19 crisis,* countries
like Greece, Spain and Italy topped the European youth unemployment
rates with 36.1 per cent, 30.6 per cent and 29.3 per cent respectively.
Surprisingly, Sweden followed in fourth place with 20.6 per cent. Due
to these percentages, people argue, erroneously, that the reasons for a
lack of jobs are because too many older people have well-paying jobs
and that the only solution is to force older people into retirement, even
if they remain highly qualified, productive and willing to work. Every
junior academic who wills the retirement of senior professors in the
hope that it will create more junior posts is falling into the lump of
labour fallacy.

In addition, organizations such as the International Monetary Fund
or the World Bank present population ageing as a ruinous societal occur-
rence or a demographic 'crisis' that will not only threaten the welfare
of older people but also that of children and grandchildren who are left
with the task of providing for older people. In some countries this has
been taken as evidence that the welfare state will become unsustainable
given the expected increased cost of health and long-term care coupled
with the comparatively small number of working adults, while in others
that the welfare state has been turned to serve the interests of older
people at the expense of the young, wrongly assuming that older people
become dependent on society after reaching a certain age. The result is
the increasing belief that politicians tend to promote short-term benefits
for older people at the expense of long-term social investment due to
intense political pressure imposed by older voters. Younger generation
voters are assuming that older people are of the 'selfish generation' as
they have been able to tailor welfare spending to meet their own needs
at the expense of future generations.

More than anything, the 'blame older people' narrative provides a
potential justification for scaling back the welfare state. If populations are
ageing, with inevitable consequences, some will view the only solution
is to tear down the welfare state. Cutting back on public services (and

therefore individualizing burdens) will reduce future public debt. Spending nothing is the most superficial route to fiscal sustainability, even if it comes with a host of undesirable effects on well-being, equity and society overall (Cooper, 2021 analyses the politicial origins of this argument).

Shifting from the arithmetic of intergenerational public transfers to broader theories that impute shared orientations to generations, we find more opportunities to pit generation against generation. It is not hard to find media, particularly from the USA and the UK, in which older people are roundly blamed for anything from climate change to Trump to Brexit.

The rhetoric of intergenerational conflict produces two related narratives. The first narrative assumes that ageing will bankrupt the welfare state. The Baby Boomers are getting older, living longer and profiting from a welfare state supported by a younger generation that will likely end up seeing very little benefit from the welfare system they are currently and heavily paying into. The second narrative assumes that older people hold a proportionately high amount of political power that they use to influence policymakers so that policies are passed in their favour. Since older people are deserving, seeing as they effectively built up the welfare state, society over-caters to them through heavy investment at the expense of younger generations. Both of these narratives end in the same place: cuts. The first leads to cuts through the implementation of austerity measures, thereby cutting welfare benefits for both older people and younger generations, while the second narrative leads to cuts for future generations as all the available welfare money goes to serving the needs of the elderly, thereby effectively leaving younger generations without certain benefits. Both create an 'us' vs. 'them' mentality in which the gain of one generation is the loss of another.

These are arguments for seeing ageing as a case of zero-sum, win-lose, politics. Policies can create win-lose intergenerational politics. The simplest example is pension system changes that leave younger people paying for a system they will not enjoy, while also having to make provisions for their own retirement. Political arguments can try to create and play on a public sense that generational politics is win-lose: the core of the 'greedy geezers' argument is precisely that people in one generation are taking too much from others. There is little natural generational tension in health politics, as we argue but political elites and policy can induce it.

1.3 Are Policy Concerns about Population Ageing Evidence-Based?

An important outstanding question is whether the policy worries about population ageing are backed up by evidence. To shed light on this, the European Observatory on Health Systems and Policies initiated a study series on the Economics of Healthy and Active Ageing. The series investigates key policy questions associated with population ageing, bringing together findings from research and country experiences. This includes reviews of what is known about the health and long-term care costs of older people, as well as many of the economic and societal benefits of healthy ageing. The series also explores policy options within the health and long-term care sectors, as well as other areas beyond the care sector, which either minimize avoidable health and long-term care costs, support older people so that they can continue to contribute meaningfully to society or otherwise contribute to the sustainability of care systems in the context of changing demographics. The evidence is quite clear that population ageing will not become a major driver of health spending trends, and that even though there will be labour market changes associated with population ageing, older people remain productive (whether they are paid or unpaid), at least to a greater extent than the data often used would suggest.

1.3.1 Population Ageing Will Not Become a Major Driver of Health Expenditure Growth

Generally, developed countries find that per person health expenditures are higher amongst older people. The superficially reasonable inference is often that increased population ageing will lead to a steep increase in health spending. One recent study (G.Williams et al., 2019) applied data on public health expenditure patterns by age to population projections for the European Union and found only an insignificant effect between health spending growth and population up until 2060. The result would add less than 1 percentage point per year to per person annual growth. The study also considered an extreme scenario wherein per person health expenditures for older people compared with their younger counterparts are significantly higher than current EU health expenditure data suggest. Even in such a scenario, population ageing only increases the overall EU health spending share of GDP by 0.85 more percentage points in 2060 compared to the baseline projection.

A review of literature (Cylus et al., 2018) found that health care costs do increase for older people right before they die, usually due to increased hospitalizations, but that this is less so the case with the 'older old' (80+). Overall, in many countries, after a certain age, the older people are when they die, the less the cost. This is perhaps due to the fact that, after a certain age, fewer resource-intensive interventions are used. This suggests that increased longevity could potentially result in an even smaller contribution to health spending growth due to population ageing than would currently be predicted.

Likewise, caring for older adults or the 'older old' is not as costly to finance as some may think, especially considering that they contribute economic and social value to society when they are healthy and active (Evans et al., 2001; Jayawardana et al., 2019). The first reason is that population ageing only gradually affects health expenditure forecasts, as opposed to cost drivers such as price growth and technological innovation, which have a substantially greater impact. Secondly, while demand for long-term care (both nursing homes and at home care) will undoubtedly increase, it will increase from a very low baseline. It was projected that the total expenditure needed for the long-term care of older adults is expected to increase by 162 per cent from 2015 to 2035 under the baseline scenario, but as a share of GDP this depicts an increase of only 1.02 per cent to 1.68 per cent (Wittenberg et al., 2018).

1.3.2 Population Ageing Will Lead to Changes in Paid and Unpaid Work, but These Can Be Managed

Cylus et al. (2018) also explained that the changes in paid and unpaid work as a result of population ageing are not necessarily unmanageable. Population ageing leads to an increase in the number of retirees, resulting in a decrease in the amount of people engaged in paid work. While this trend is unavoidable, there are four points that suggest it is unlikely to spell catastrophe for societies. The first is that some older adults choose to continue participating in the paid workforce well after they have retired, which is beneficial as they continue to contribute to a society's economic output. The second point shows that while it is true that older people's consumption is predominantly financed through public transfers, there are many older adults that pay for (part of) their consumption through private sources (either through a contin-ued income from work or through accumulated assets). Health is a key predictor of asset accumulation; people in poor health are unable to accumulate substantial assets throughout their life-course as they have shorter life expectancies, lower earnings and higher out-of-pocket health care costs, highlighting that keeping older adults in good health is exceptionally important. Third, even if older adults are not in paid employment, they still pay consumption and non-labour-related taxes, thereby contributing to public-sector revenues. Finally, there are many unpaid workers, particularly older adults, who still produce outputs that generate economic and social value. A generally invisible non-market-based output is that of an informal caregiver. These caregivers can be young adults caring for an older family member or older adults caring for either grandchildren or the 'older old'. The societal value of such unpaid work is substantial but not regularly quantified, and therefore generally goes unrecognized.

1.4 The Coronavirus Pandemic: Intergenerational Conflict or Revealing Consequences of Longstanding Inequalities?

The 2020 coronavirus global pandemic is a very recent and clear example of the political choices that could pit generations against each other. As the pandemic swept the world, governments had to walk a narrow path (Greer et al., 2020; Rajan et al., 2020): manage the pandemic using public health measures such as business restrictions to slow spread, while cushioning the economic blow with expansive social policy. This bought time for governments to build systems to test, trace, isolate, and support people, to attain something like normal society by the end of 2020. Most governments did not manage to stay on this narrow path, and instead fell into making tradeoffs between the economy and public health (Greer et al., 2021). The inequalities in COVID-19 mortality in rich countries often meant political debates about how to value the lives of older people against the putative economic benefits of early reopening.

The stakes are made much higher by the needless and tragic tradeoffs between people in the COVID-19 pandemic. As a US newspaper columnist wrote, it mattered greatly whether we highlighted the age effects of the pandemic, calling it a 'boomer remover', or the race, class and gender inequalities it revealed, which in the case of the USA made it a 'brother killer' afflicting Black men (Blow, 2020). The same exercise could be done for any country. The virus targets people unequally. The odds of catching it vary with employment and reflect inequalities: once the virus is circulating in a population, the people most at risk of catching it are those who are in constant contact with others, in confined spaces, for long periods of time. That explains why abattoirs, prisons and nursing homes were all hot spots in many places. The key inequalities there are not about age; they are about who works in 'essential' tasks, such as caring work, that are often poorly paid and largely carried out by women, people of colour and immigrants. They are also about crowded and multigenerational living arrangements where it is hard to block spread within a household. Crowding and multigenerational family living arrangements are not evenly distributed in the population. Even among nursing homes in the USA, ones with more Black and Latino patients had higher infection and mortality rates (Curtis, 2020). The risk of hospitalization and death from the virus, then, varied with age and other co-morbidities such as hypertension and diabetes. Again, these reflect other inequalities such as class, race and ethnicity. COVID-19 is clearly more dangerous to older people, but the odds of catching it and having the other co-morbidities that make it more dangerous are all reflective of deeper social inequalities from which age is mostly a distraction. COVID-19 belies simple narratives of win-lose intergenerational politics and policies. Not only did the deaths in homes for older people remind us of how poorly treated many of them are, it also showed that for all the intergenerational enmity pundits discuss, younger people were willing to stay home for them.

1.5 Win-Win Policy and Politics: the Life-Course Approach

What is the alternative to a zero-sum politics of ageing? We argue for win-win policies. Win-win policies aim for a positive-sum collective outcome, and the analytical tool that is most useful in identifying positive-sum collective outcomes in health and ageing issues is the life-course approach. Ageing is a process that takes place over a lifetime, beginning before birth and ending upon death. Nor is it a static process specific to a certain age group. Rather, it is a continuous development throughout one's lifetime (Kalache & Kickbusch, 1997). In order to better see the case of ageing as such, a life-course concept was developed. This is a holistic examination of the various life stages, beginning with embryonic and foetal life, infancy, early childhood, school age, adolescence and reproductive age (including pre-conception), all the way up to old age (Aagaard-Hansen et al., 2019). Life-course approaches are sometimes misunderstood to simply mean that we should focus on the very young, but understood correctly a life-course perspective identifies positive interventions at every age. The life-course perspective not only shows that a person's current health is shaped by early exposures to physical, environmental and psychological factors (Jones et al., 2019), but also helps in understanding the origin, persistence and transmission of health disparities across generations (Braveman, 2009; Kuh et al., 2003).

In order to be able to address transgenerational disparities and the disadvantages they bring with them, interventions need to envelop multi-generations, which implies looking towards all-encompassing solutions such as universal primary prevention, strengthening families and building children's skills through adolescence and young adulthood (Jones et al., 2019). With every child able to reach his or her potential to be a healthy, engaged, productive citizen, the skills to plan for and parent the next generation are secured (Cheng et al., 2016). In this way, a life-course perspective is incorporated into health disparities interventions by seeing the whole person, the entire family and the comprehensive community system (Cheng & Solomon, 2014).

If the goal is healthy ageing, then policies and initiatives must encourage the healthy development of the individual so that human capital can be accumulated and maintained over the course of one's life (Bovenberg, 2007). The ultimate goal of the life-course perspective is to help individuals maintain the highest possible level of functional capacity throughout all stages of their life while reducing inequalities not only between gender and classes, but also between the generations (Anxo et al., 2010).

The World Health Organization presents an action framework for policymakers that helps visualize the investments necessary within the various stages (WHO, 2007) while at the same time recognizing the connections across all stages and domains in life (Maeder, 2015). According to the Minsk Declaration assembled at the WHO European ministerial conference in Belarus in 2015 (WHO, 2015), an *adaptation of a life-course approach* in the context of health means the following:

- recognizing that all stages of a person's life are intricately intertwined with each other, with the lives of other people in society and with past and future generations of their families;
- understanding that health and wellbeing depend on interactions between risk and protective factors throughout people's lives;

- taking action… early to ensure the best start in life; appropriately to protect and promote health during life's transition periods; and together, as a whole society, to create healthy environments, improve conditions of daily life and strengthen people-centred health systems.

Successful applications of the life-course approach can be found in the initiatives brought forth by Iceland surrounding the economic crisis and its impact on welfare, as well as by Malta and its confrontation of obesity and its direct costs to the health care system.

Box 1.1 Icelandic Welfare Watch

ICELANDIC WELFARE WATCH

Problem: The initiative was established as a response to the Icelandic financial crisis in 2008 where the three largest banks collapsed, the national currency fell by 86 per cent, unemployment rose from 2 to 8 per cent and inflation increased from 6 to 18 per cent. This crisis caused major stress on public budgets whereby public authorities were made to operate under highly constrained conditions.

Initiative Aim: The objective was to create a system that could reduce the impact of health-related problems when a society was hit by economic collapse. This strategy included limiting the negative impact of the crisis on populations' wellbeing, developing emergency responses and services for different social groups in situations of crisis and creating flexible employment solutions.

Life-Course Approach: Working groups were established to help children and families with children to ensure sufficient access to relevant services such as guaranteed school lunches. Additional working groups were developed to create social indicators responsible for tracking welfare across social groups over time with the goal of monitoring and informing policies and services. Furthermore, a steering group made up of local authorities, health service workers, ministers, etc., was created to implement measures to support households, draft guidelines for local authorities on budget reduction and define basic welfare and educational services.

Sources: CHRODIS, n.d.; WHO, 2018; Whittaker & Thorsteinsson, 2016

Box 1.2 Healthy Weight for Life strategy

HEALTHY WEIGHT FOR LIFE STRATEGY (HWL)
DEVELOPED BY *MALTA*

Problem: The initiative was established in response to the immense problem of obesity in Malta, where 40–48 per cent of children and 58 per cent of adults are overweight and obese. This produces an excess direct cost for the Maltese health service estimated at €20 million per year, and amounted to 5.7 per cent of the country's total health expenditure in 2008.

Initiative Aim: The overall aim of the HWL strategy is to curb and reverse the growing proportion of overweight and obese children and adults in the population in order to reduce the health, social and economic consequences of excess bodyweight.

Life-Course Approach: Promoting healthy eating in early years through the increased encouragement of breastfeeding and during a child's school years through the use of school-wide competitions and guidelines for parents, but also at the workplace and in homes for the elderly. Incentives to encourage a higher intake of fruits and vegetables were implemented in 2011 and incentives for employers were established to foster healthy eating at the workplace. The introduction of hospital-wide regulations to ensure that canteens in hospitals and homes for elderly adults are following healthy dietary guidelines.

Sources: Superintendence of Public Health, 2012; WHO, 2018

1.6 The Book in Brief

Many will argue that the reason societies don't opt for win-win solutions is the selfish interests of older people; in other words, that we get win-lose policies because of win-lose politics, and it's older people who sustain those politics. The argument runs that their numerical weight and political engagement mean that politicians attend to their interests, and that their interests are in generous benefits for themselves, paid for in ways that damage the interests of younger people. We argue in Chapter 3 that this argument is simply wrong in most countries. Even in the United States and United Kingdom, where it is probably most valid, it is not a very useful explanation of politics and policy. Older people are far more diverse than such an image suggests, and they do not vote as a bloc. In fact, many are generous to younger people, in their personal actions and in their politics. As common sense and our lived experience would suggest, many older people are very concerned for the welfare of their families and their societies. Thus, for example, it is perfectly coherent for older people to have voted on issues such as Brexit; a vote for either Leave or Remain could be intended as a vote to leave a better country for future generations. To say that older people should vote differently or not vote is to devalue their experience and assume their absolute egoism: a manifest error. Older people do not vote as a bloc because, as individuals, their lives are shaped by many other factors that are more important than age: class, gender, ethnicity, nationality, rurality, family status and all the other factors that cumulate into an individual voter's approach to the world.

Even if an older persons' bloc vote did exist, there is actually no reason to expect that politicians would listen to it. This might come as a surprise to those who expect politicians to chase the median voter (aka the centre of the electorate) but is borne out by a great deal of political science research. Chapter 4 shows that there is very little political science research suggesting that policies of any kind are driven by electoral demand. Rather, policy is shaped by factors primarily of interest to elites (e.g. a perception of fiscal unsustainability, or EU law or international advice), interest group activities (e.g. the lobbying of unions, employers and others) and internal arguments among senior politicians about what strategies to pursue in order to win elections. Collectively, these elite interests and coalitions shape the policies and agendas offered to voters (Greer, 2015; Kingdon, 2010). The preferences of the putative median voters can change with framing and agenda-setting, which is why median voter models are essentially misleading. This is a point with vast supporting evidence in political science, but one that runs contrary to comfortable ideas about politicians 'pandering' (Jacobs & Shapiro, 2000), and also runs contrary to comfortable ideas that modern democratic political systems make decisions that reflect exogenous voters' views rather than complex interest politics in which public opinions and elections are only one, malleable, component (Hacker & Pierson, 2014). We should not focus the blame on voters of any age if they are primarily responding to agendas set by others.

If elite supply of policy ideas rather than voters' demand for electoral ideas shapes the agenda and the decisions, then the road to understanding decisions about ageing and health starts with understanding the supply of ideas. Chapter 5 focuses on the politics of the supply of ideas. Policies can powerfully shape the way that individual people, geographic places and larger polities experience demographic changes and the ensuing politics. It shows that there are multiple, complex, ways in which coalitions can come together to produce win-win solutions. Women's organizations, public sector unions and providers of health and long-term care all appear as advocates for life-course approaches to ageing. This reflects their interests: for example, organizations representing the largely female and often precarious long-term care workforce might have an interest in expanded access and funding for care services, while working women might appreciate assistance with their caring responsibilities. Universal long-term care, for example, might be championed by a coalition of employers, unions and women's organizations who want to keep working-age female employees in the labour force instead of having them drop out to focus on caring, providers and unions of their employees who seek a stable source of funding for their businesses, local governments eager to dispose of expensive responsibilities to care for indigent older people, and a finance ministry concerned about the loss of working age women to the unpaid care sector. An option thus formulated could then be put to voters in the expectation that many people, such as working women, would like it. Indeed, this is almost exactly what happened in Japan (Schoppa, 2006).

These two chapters, together, make a key claim of this book: age, however understood, is a weak predictor of anything to do with the politics of ageing. Once rigorous controls for variables such as education, income and wealth have been introduced, age itself is a weak predictor of people's opinions, and public opinion is a weak predictor of politics. Instead of drawing facile lines from demographics through interests and public opinion to policies, it makes more sense to reverse the direction of causality and understand policy decisions and agendas as the product of arguments among and within coalitions of elites and interests. Organized groups such as political parties, employers, unions, the finance sector (insurers), women's organizations and organizations that represent older people shape policy ideas, political strategies and the definition of problems (Greer, 2015).

Framing the politics of ageing as a war of the generations obscures what really shapes the lives and views of older as well as younger people. Chapter 6 reframes the stakes of ageing politics, arguing that the real question of ageing in politics and health should be: who gets to be old? The 'Greedy Geezer' narrative of self-serving older people implicitly focuses our attention on wealthy older people, summoning an image of people who retire early to spend decades on cruise ships, and obscuring the experiences and problems of those who are not so lucky. What truth it has comes from the simple fact that many of the least lucky, the people who are most affected by health and broader socioeconomic inequalities, don't get to be old. Systemic inequities in societies are reflected in health data, which includes both life expectancy and healthy life expectancy. There are many policies that have some ability to reduce health inequalities, typically through reducing broader inequalities.

As sports commentators say, it is important to keep one's eye on the ball. Consider a basic thought experiment in the social policy of ageing. If we argue that universal public long-term care is unaffordable, all we propose to do is change the ways in which long-term care is provided for most people. If we finance long-term care out-of-pocket, we can expect the predictable effects of any shift of social expenditure to out-of-pocket payments. The very wealthy might not see much change. Middle-class families with some patrimony will see the costs of care eat into their inheritances. Working-class families will probably see a reduction in their disposable income, whether they spend it on care provision or have a family member reduce their participation in paid employment in order to provide informal care. For the unluckiest, old age will mean whatever system exists in a given country to look after the indigent. As COVID19 hotspots in nursing homes show, that system is usually not set up to maximize older people's wellbeing. On the other hand, if we establish a public universal system, it will concentrate a very large expenditure into one programme, and while that programme might be attractive, it will also contain intimidating upfront costs. Those groups in society, especially high-earning individuals who do not expect to benefit but do expect to pay for it in their taxes, will be opponents, even if it is in principle an efficient way to maximize overall social welfare by ensuring that everybody has a guarantee of decent long-term care, financed by the broadest possible pool. As this stylized example might make clear, *the distributional decisions are not intergenerational. They are intra-generational, deciding how resources will be allocated between classes.*

Chapter 7 keeps our eye on the ball, evaluating the inequality dynamics of two different events: German Reunification and the rise of

English investment in reducing inequalities under Labour governments (1996–2010) followed by its fall under Conservative-led governments since 2010. These two very different events both produced discontinuities which allowed us to understand the impact of win-win (positive sum) or win-lose (zero-sum) policies on who even gets to be old, let alone live well. Inequalities can be reduced, but the effective way to reduce them is by focusing not on putative intergenerational inequalities but rather on more deeply rooted inequalities that reproduce across generations and are made up of more than the legacies of the political economies that people occupied when they were younger.

The conclusion points back to the extent to which the talk of an 'ageing crisis' that so preoccupies many policy analysts despite its scant empirical foundations has shaped the supply side of policies. Zombie ideas such as 'ageing societies face increased health care costs' continue to march along despite multiple efforts to kill them off. In the face of those zombie ideas, this chapter argues that real-life studies show how policies that use life-course approaches to achieve equity make real differences, and the kind of austerity favoured by many advocates of intergenerational accounting actively harms society.

1.7 Conclusion

Much of the global discourse about ageing and health is needlessly gloomy. One of the great postwar achievements, the welfare state, has enabled another wondrous outcome: a human society in which most people live for a long time. But for some, these two goals are now in conflict, and the ageing society makes the welfare state that helped birth it unsustainable. Some view many of the aforementioned threats as unavoidable and unsolvable and conclude that the only remedy is to tear down the welfare state, dismantle entitlement programmes and raise retirement ages. What should be viewed as one of social policy's greatest achievements is instead the impetus for its destruction.

Ageing as a health policy problem is very manageable, and there is lots of good research and policy thinking on topics such as the best way to recalibrate primary care services to respond to ageing populations. As shown above, there is also little reason to expect that ageing societies will have substantially higher health care costs, or even that we are measuring everything that matters, given the role of older people in informal care, civil society and other unpaid roles that often conflict with paid employment but are crucial to people, families and societies.

It might be surprising to learn that ageing is not necessarily a big problem for the fiscal sustainability of health systems; it might also be surprising to learn that the politics of ageing are not necessarily the politics of intergenerational warfare. Not only are win-win solutions possible, that are beneficial all along the life-course, but the politics of those solutions are more concrete and personal than airy talk of generations suggests. On one side, voters have concrete and personal experiences and interests, born of experiences as disparate as dropping out of paid employment to care for parents and depending on parents' caring in order to work. Those experiences do not translate in any simple way into a demand for greater or lesser taxes or social expenditures. People can be generous as well as selfish, and even if they are selfish, they will often define their selfishness in terms of their family, locale, race, ethnicity or class rather than age. Elites, meanwhile, are paid to represent groups, shape agendas and make policy, and have much more specific interests, whether they represent doctors, care homes, the elderly, workers, women, the finance ministry or any of the many other groups seeking advantage in the politics of ageing societies. Those elites' interactions, and the coalitions and conflicts among them, shape what policies are offered to voters and what drive politics.

This book brings together research on why population ageing is often (erroneously) viewed cataclysmically, particularly from a health financing perspective, and reviews approaches to get the win-win ageing policies we need. The 'crisis' that Western Europe is facing is not so much that demographics are shifting as that there are currently few sufficient and effective policies in place to support the shift in a sustainable way. Ageing societies are not doomed to crisis, or even to difficulties sustaining their welfare state. There are win-win solutions, which can be inferred from a life-course approach, but they often require overcoming narrow interests by building broader coalitions.

The <u>controversy</u> that this book speaks to is the general belief that wealthy older people, assumed to be a homogeneous voting group, vote for policies that benefit themselves; this is a falsity depicted both demographically and theoretically. Older people do not vote homogeneously and in most polities policy is only partially a product of electoral demands. In addition, as shown briefly in this chapter, it is incorrect to think that all older people are poor, but at the same time not all of them are rich; this is a very heterogeneous group, which also makes them very susceptible to inequalities. Given the heterogeneity among older people there are some that may need support; this support is not that expensive and can be made intergenerationally fair through the implementation of not ageing policies but life-course policies.

Coalitions are the result of intersecting solidarities: intergenerational and class as well as citizenship and gender. Coalitions are the answer to establishing healthy ageing policies without sacrificing people of any age. Policymakers need to understand how gender, class and region collectively shape ageing politics in order to be able to understand the tradeoffs in place. Only with this understanding can equitable and effective win-win policies be made.

The argument that the book makes is a simple one: Western societies can evolve from the politics of unhealthy ageing produced by lose-lose policies to the politics of healthy ageing by following a life-course approach through the adaptation of win-win policies. The aim is to solve the "ageing crisis" in the same it way it was created: politics. We argue that using political imagination can point us to policies which decrease both inter- and intragenerational inequalities.

2 | *Older People in Europe*

2.1 Diversity and Inequality

We too often form our perspectives or design policies based on simplistic notions of generational warfare or stereotypes. Precise definitions and examination of data on the life conditions of older people lead us to the same conclusion as a quick contemplation of our own lives: the situations, goals and behaviours of older people are very diverse.

Defining older people is not simple. Even though population ageing is something that clearly occurs due to shifts in age-demographics in their entirety (i.e. increases in the number of people at older ages relative to the number of people at younger ages), when we talk about population ageing – and especially when we warn of the consequences of population ageing – usually we are really focusing our attention on older people. To understand then the consequences of population ageing it makes sense to turn our attention to focus primarily on the people that make up this group. It must be acknowledged that there is no age grouping that universally defines people as being older. Often (as we will discuss further below) age 65 is taken as a cut-off point, with anyone above age 65 being considered older. In fact, the diversity of the ageing experience can be divided to encompass 'older adults' (65–84) and the 'older old' (85+). These categories can be further divided by including the 'younger old' (65–74), but for the purposes of this book the two categories will suffice. As lived experience shows, calendar age is a convenient way to classify but a poor guide to health status or behaviour. People at the same age have varying degrees of health and activity, which ultimately affects their role in society.

Further, discussions of ageing societies do not always distinguish between different interpretations of what different cohort (generation) sizes mean. It is possible to discuss simple numbers: more people were born in year X than in year Y. This means, for example, that the size of the Baby Boom generation (the generation born just after World

War Two) affects pension expenditures, while the relatively small size of the generation born after the mid-1990s is producing a decline in demand for education in many places. These are simple demographic facts that we can see in Figure 1.2. Their actual policy impact is not so simple, though, and depends on other factors. For example, people born after the mid-1990s might be less numerous, but various factors including policy might encourage a higher share of them to pursue higher education. It is also possible to identify patterns in which a given property is more common in a given cohort. Higher education became much more accessible in the UK over the postwar years, which produces a relationship between age and likelihood that a person is a graduate. People who entered the labour market in a major downturn such as that of 2008 often face lower lifetime earnings. As we will argue, these relationships are more complex than they sound because they are shot through with intragenerational inequalities. Third, and perhaps most ambitious, are analyses that try to attribute a cast of mind to an entire generation. They channel the intuition in the quote attributed to Napoleon Bonaparte: 'To understand the man you have to know what was happening in the world when he was twenty.' These analyses (e.g. Howe & Strauss, 1992, 2009), which turn generations into actors, are generally based on shared formative characteristics; for example, the Baby Boomers or Millennials purportedly developed shared political and cultural ideas because of their shared experiences. They are far more problematic, as we shall argue below, because they privilege one variable, age, over all the other things that shape people's life experiences and views. Many of them almost immediately disqualify themselves because a close reading shows the partiality of the viewpoints they impressionistically represent (most often well off and highly educated ones) and the tendentiousness of their arguments (Bristow, 2019). Any account that gives the impression that most people have attended university, still less an elite university, gives away its own unrepresentativeness.

Distinguishing between these three understandings of generations matters greatly: it is not the same thing to say that 'there are more 45–49 year olds than 25–29 year olds in a given country' (an ascertainable demographic fact), to say that '35 year olds have on average lower average earnings than 45 year olds did at the same age' (already a more probabilistic statement), and to say that '35 year olds are more likely to share a particular understanding of politics and policy that fferent from 45 year olds after controlling for other factors' (an itious statement indeed).

_t is, nonetheless, easy to slide between the three different understandings of demographics, but doing so can mislead because the experiences of people are very diverse within and between cohorts, and often more appropriately explained by other factors. Empirically, we do indeed find that the lived experiences of older people are different, within and between countries and within and between cohorts. The following sections intend to illustrate the experience of being an older person in European countries in 2017 using the 7th wave of SHARE[1].

2.1.1 Income Insecurity Varies across the European Region, but It Is Better to Be on the Margins in Northern & Western Europe Than in Eastern Europe

Wealth has a considerable impact on whether healthy ageing is likely and whether ageing populations have a positive or negative impact on society. Wealthy men and women not only live longer, they also get more healthy life years after 50 years of age than the poorest individuals (Zaninotto et al., 2020). In addition, the researchers found that education and social class also had an impact, but wealth was by far more significant. Similarly, wealthy older adults have a more positive impact on society than their poorer counterparts simply because they are healthier, thereby requiring less intensive or expensive care. In addition they were able to accumulate more asset wealth, which in turn contributed to economic growth when the assets translated into capital investments (Cylus et al., 2018).

An important concern at older ages therefore is income insecurity. While there are worries about the sustainability of pension systems in many country contexts, other countries have limited or non-existent pensions, causing older people to struggle to make ends meet. According to SHARE data, the extent to which older people age 65 and above

---

[1] According to its website, 'The Survey of Health, Ageing and Retirement in Europe (SHARE) is a multidisciplinary and cross-national panel database of micro data on health, socioeconomic status and social and family networks of about 140,000 individuals aged 50 or older (around 380,000 interviews). SHARE covers 27 European countries and Israel.' In this chapter we use data from the 7th and most recent wave of SHARE, which includes data collected in 2017.

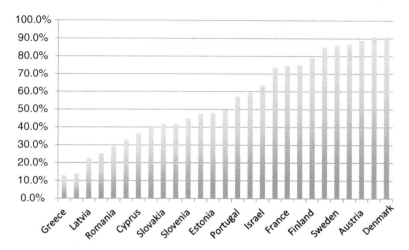

Figure 2.1 Percentage of people age 65+ who report they are able to make ends meet.

report that they feel they are able to make ends meet varies across countries, from 13 per cent in Greece and Bulgaria to 91 per cent in Denmark and Luxembourg (Figure 2.1).

Grouping countries regionally into Southern Europe, Eastern Europe and Northern & Western Europe highlights the broad differences. For example, 85 per cent of people over age 65 in Northern & Western Europe reported they could easily or fairly easily get by, while only 58 per cent and 39 per cent respectively in Southern and Eastern Europe reported the same. Even controlling for differences in age and gender[2] among the SHARE respondents, the probability of a person over age 65 feeling unable to meet basic needs in Southern Europe is over four times higher than in Northern & Western Europe and over nine times higher in Eastern Europe than in Northern & Western Europe.

Within these broad regions, there are still significant differences in income insecurity. Less educated (ISCED-1997 below level 3) older people in general are more likely to face income insecurities, no matter where they live. But a low educated person in a country where a greater percentage of older people do not experience income insecurity is still

[2] All models in this chapter are logit models that control for age, age[2] (to capture some degree of non-linearity) and gender unless described otherwise. Data are weighted using population weights.

better off than a low educated person in a country where the majority of older people do experience income security.

Looking only at the Northern & Western Europe sample as a whole, again adjusting for age and gender, an over 65 year old with low education is more than three times more likely than a highly educated older person from Northern & Western Europe to report being unable to make ends meet. The same is true within Southern and Eastern Europe, comparing older people of different education levels, with statistically similar odds. So, within regions in Europe, the relationships between education level and income security at older ages is fairly consistent: more educated older people have greater income security.

However, comparing across all regions and levels of education together, and still controlling for age and gender, it becomes clear that a low educated older person in Northern & Western Europe on average still has greater income security than a relatively more educated person living further to the East. Model results confirm that a highly educated person 65 years and over in Eastern Europe is still more than twice as likely to feel unable to make ends meet as a low educated 65+ in Northern & Western Europe. Simply put, when it comes to income security among older people, while there are differences everywhere that vary by education, it is more favourable to grow old in some countries than it is in others.

2.1.2 Most Older People Are Not in Paid Work but the Odds of Not Working Are Higher in Eastern Europe Than in Northern and Western Europe

To compensate for the lack of pensions, in some countries older people may engage in paid work for longer. Alternatively, it may be that people who have jobs that are limited by age-related factors (e.g. construction workers) leave the labour force at comparatively younger ages, while those in office jobs or other occupations that are not so physically demanding are able to continue to work at older ages; in this way, it may end up that the people who work longer are those who are more well off, rather than those who need to do so.

According to the SHARE data, the percentage of people above 65 working is overall quite low, around 2.5 per cent. This varies from 0.1 per cent in Romania to 18 per cent in Israel, though in most countries the percentage is below 5 per cent. Most people in Europe are retired by the time they reach age 65.

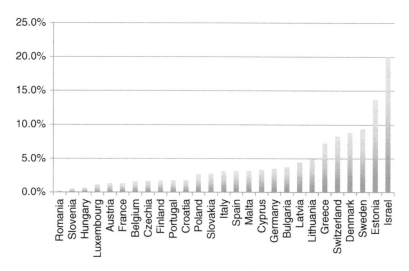

Figure 2.2 Percentage of people age 65+ who are in paid work.

In fact, the likelihood of working after age 65 is much lower for Eastern Europeans than it is for the rest of Europe (Figure 2.2). Models suggest that Eastern Europeans over age 65 are more than twice as likely as Northern & Western Europeans to be retired or otherwise not working as opposed to working. This suggests that the ability to work is probably more of a luxury rather than something that older people continue to do in order to make ends meet.

2.1.3 Older People in Eastern Europe Are Most Likely to Live in Multigenerational Households

Who older people live with is important for understanding their level of support. Older people are at an age where their children (if they have them) are adults. In some countries they will have left the family home, while in others adult children may stay until they are married. In others, multigenerational households may be the norm.

Looking at the SHARE data, 56 per cent of respondents age 65 and over reported living with their spouse or partner. The lowest percentages of respondents living with their spouse or partner is in Eastern Europe, compared to Northern & Western Europe and Southern Europe. A likely explanation for this is lower life expectancies in Eastern Europe, so the region is likely to have more widows or widowers. Models ıggest older people in Northern & Western Europe are 1.4 times and n Southern Europe 1.7 times as likely as Eastern Europeans to live with their spouse or partner.

However, older Eastern Europeans, on average, also have the largest households. According to the age 65 and over respondents in the SHARE data, the average household size in Northern & Western Europe is 1.7 people, compared to 1.9 people in Southern Europe and 2.1 people in Eastern Europe.

In fact, defining multigenerational households as any household with more than two people, or those with two people where the respondent reports not living with a spouse or partner, there is a much higher likelihood of Eastern European older people living in multigenerational households than older people in other regions. According to model estimates, an older person in Eastern Europe is more than 5 times as likely as an older person in Northern & Western Europe to live in a multigenerational household. Southern European older people are around 3.5 times as likely as an older person in Northern & Western Europe to live in a multigenerational household.

2.1.4 *The Health of Older People Varies across Regions*

Health (and, similarly, disability) is exceptionally important to consider when thinking about the ageing population. A key question that must be understood within this context is whether older people are spending their later years in good or bad health. This is significant because if longer life is healthy, active and fulfilling, then population ageing is less likely to become a potential crisis. If, however, ageing corresponds to a longer period of illness and limited activity, economic, social and health care costs may increase once a greater share of the population reaches older ages. The latest assessment of the health of older people in Europe (Rechel et al., 2020) finds that the assessment of whether people live longer in better or worse health depends very much on the measures used. In addition, the differences between and within countries are substantial, making it difficult to speculate on overall trends. The takeaway message is that while it is difficult to make broad statements about the health and disability trends among older people, health systems have the potential to contribute to increases in life expectancies, decreases in severe disability, and better coping and functioning with chronic disease.

Health status is notoriously difficult to compare across individuals. Self-reported health status is one of the most commonly used indicators, despite the potential for reporting biases. Self-reported health is reported in SHARE on a 1–5 scale (1 is excellent, 5 is poor). For convenience we convert this into a binary indicator of good health.

The percentage of people over age 65 reporting good health differs across countries. Fewer than a third of older people over age 65 in Estonia, Latvia, Lithuania and Hungary report good health, whereas more than two-thirds of older people over age 65 in Sweden, Belgium, Czechia, Denmark and Switzerland report good health. Unsurprisingly, again the differences among older people can be seen very clearly looking across broad regions: 54 per cent of Northern & Western Europeans over age 65 report good health, 49 per cent of Southern Europeans, and only 40 per cent of Eastern Europeans.

These differences highlight very clearly how calendar age does not tell the full story when it comes to the life experience of being an older person. Controlling for gender, logit models suggest that the odds of 65–69 year olds in Northern & Western Europe reporting good health (as opposed to poor health) does not statistically differ from their same-aged counterparts in Southern Europe. But 65–69 year olds from Northern & Western Europe are nearly 70 per cent more likely to report good health than 65–69 year olds in Eastern Europe (Figure 2.3).

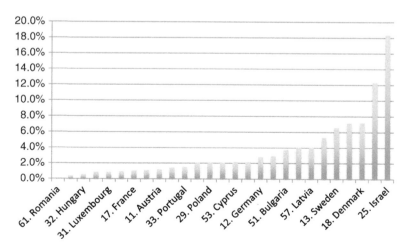

Figure 2.3 Percentage of people age 65+ who report good health.

Put another way, the same models estimate that the odds of an Eastern European 65–69 year old reporting to be in good health are not statistically different from a 75–79 year old in Northern & Western Europe reporting to be in good health. Effectively one could interpret this to mean that when it comes to self-reported health, Eastern Europeans, on average, age about a decade ahead of Northern & Western Europeans by the time they are in their late 60s.

Of course, it isn't only the region where an older person lives that matters for their health. Even after accounting for the effects of living in a particular region, more educated older people everywhere still have better odds of ageing in good health than those who are less educated. Figure 2.4 reports the odds of reporting good health by age and education (all relative to 65–69 year olds who have low levels of education). The odds ratios are shown in line graphs to help to visualize how the likelihood of reporting good health changes with age. Controlling for gender and region, across all education levels, the likelihood of reporting good health declines with age. But because the odds decline from different starting points, more educated people retain a health advantage. For example, a highly educated 65–69-year-old European is 1.5 times more likely to report that they are in good health compared to a low educated 65–69 year old. A highly educated 75–79 year old also has a likelihood of reporting good health that is statistically not different

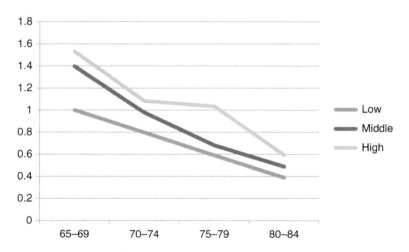

Figure 2.4 Predicted odds of reporting good health by age category and level of education.

from the odds of a low educated 65–69 year old reporting good health. What this implies is that after controlling for the effects of living in a particular region, low educated people in their late 60s have effectively aged – at least when it comes to their self-reported health – about ten years faster than those with high levels of education.

2.2 What Do Commonly Used Data Say about Population Ageing and Its Effects on Society?

The above analysis illustrates what many would think is obvious and which the late singer Aaliyah said even more succinctly in 1994 at the age of 15: 'age ain't nothing but a number'. Older people may share common traits but, depending on factors including (but not limited to) their education and the country they live in, they often have very different experiences in terms of their income security, support networks and health status. In effect, age, while not completely insignificant, is not necessarily the most important predictor when it comes to many factors, simply because what it means to age for different people in different country contexts differs.

Highlighting this variability among older people matters, because all too often policies that are considered when trying to respond to the perceived threats of population ageing take a broad-brush approach. Whether proposing to deal with fiscal pressures by raising pension ages across the board or resisting calls to expand entitlement to long-term or social care services without acknowledging the huge variation in access to informal care or abilities to self-fund social care, all too often older people are treated like a single homogeneous group.

Nevertheless, many of the common metrics used in the context of population ageing do not take these differences across older people into account. At face value, some of them would seem to support concerns over population ageing. One of the most well-known metrics is known as the old-age dependency ratio, sometimes referred to as a support ratio. These aim to compare the ratio of the 'non-working' population to the 'working' population by relating the size of the population above a pre-determined chronological age (considered not to be working and to require 'support') to the adult population below the pre-determined age (who are considered to be working and thus 'supporting' them). For example, one could calculate the ratio of the population size over 65 years to the population size 15–64 years and express the ratio per

100 working-age people (e.g. 30 older people for every 100 of working age). The age threshold is often 65, which reflects the official pension age in many countries.

Despite its ubiquities, this metric has a number of important limitations. Chief among these is the assumption that all older people above a certain age are out of work, requiring and in receipt of external financial support, while younger-aged adults are assumed to be economically active and contributing into support systems. In fact, there is considerable variability in terms of normal retirement ages (i.e. the official age at which an individual can retire with a full pension) and average effective retirement ages (i.e. the age of exit from the labour force), both across countries and within countries across time, as well as between men and women. For example, according to OECD data, in South Korea men work on average 11.0 years beyond their normal retirement age, whereas in Slovenia men leave the labour force on average 5.4 years before their normal retirement age. Women in South Korea work 11.2 years longer, while women in Poland leave the labour force 7.2 years before normal retirement age.

Data from 1970 to 2014 also suggest that across countries, people have been leaving the formal labour force at progressively earlier ages over time, with a slight reversal to that trend in recent years (see Figure 2.5). The OECD-34 average retirement age for men in 1970 was 68.4 years, but this fell to a low of 63 years by 2004 before slowly rising again to 65.1 years in 2016.

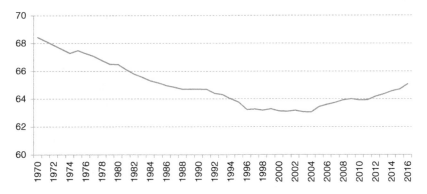

Figure 2.5 Average retirement ages among men in OECD-34 countries, 1970 to 2016.

Source: Cylus et al., 2019

Using any single age threshold for the support ratio will mask the fact that many people above the age threshold remain in the workforce, particularly in low-income countries, and many other older people who are not in the workforce are economically independent, are not dependent on the state for their incomes and pay tax on asset-based income and pensions. Not all younger people below the age threshold are economically active; as of April 2020, seasonally adjusted youth unemployment (under 25 years) was 15.8 per cent in the Eurozone (Eurostat, 2020). Increases in working-age unemployment rates increase the ratio of those who are genuinely dependent to those who are supporting them. This is a particular problem given high youth unemployment in many countries – but has no effect on the support ratio metric itself.

In essence, the old-age support ratio seems to raise an important policy question: will the older portion of the population become so large that it is unsustainable to continue to support it in the same way as before? It is a strangely simplistic concept. To say, in isolation, that we should be worried about the dependency ratio is to ignore productivity (if one working person is three times as productive as her grandparents, then why can't she support three times more dependents?), the reduction in education and early years expenditure that arithmetically is happening when a society 'ages', and the uncounted contributions made by older people (e.g. unpaid child care that enables working age people's labour market participation while probably also contributing to the health and happiness of children).

Even if we put aside these basic conceptual problems with dependency ratios, the challenge is determining how most accurately to capture the comparison between the size of the population requiring support and the size of the supporting population. There are additional caveats to consider, including the fact that the supported population may be supporting itself to some extent through its own taxes, through providing informal care for other people requiring support, or through income from savings and assets. Two alternative approaches attempt more properly to account for changes in population health and disability, and for changes in the proportion of consumers and producers.

Accounting for health and disability can be done through a metric called the prospective old-age dependency ratio (POADR), which takes forecasted increases in life expectancy into account and is defined as the number of people in age groups with life expectancies of fifteen years or fewer, divided by the number of people aged 20 years or older

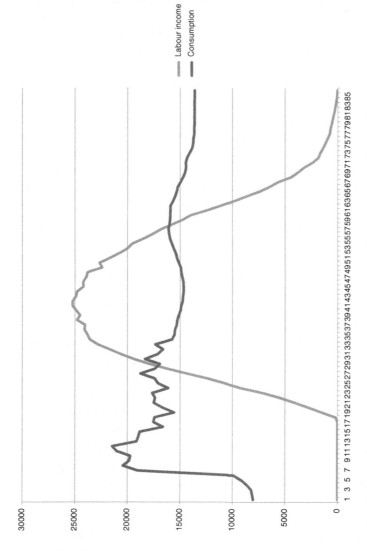

Figure 2.6 Labour income and consumption over the life-cycle, South Korea, 2012.

Source: National Transfer Accounts, 2012

in age groups with life expectancies greater than fifteen years. Another similar option to adjust for disability is the adult disability dependency ratio (ADDR), which is the number of adults at least 20 years old with disabilities divided by the number of adults at least 20 years old without them.

Alternatively, we can also gauge the level of 'dependency' by accounting for the actual numbers of consumers and producers in the old-age dependency ratio. The National Transfer Accounts – country level data which contain information on economic flows from one age group or generation to another – can be used for this purpose. Figure 2.6 provides the intuition for this metric. Here, we can see how production and consumption vary per person across the life-course using data from South Korea as an example. In childhood, people naturally consume far in excess of their production since the majority do not engage in any sort of labour until at least their mid- to late teenage years. During traditional working years people produce far more than they are able to consume. However, as people age, their production on average begins to fall, eventually to a point where it is below their level of consumption. It follows then that a large share of the population at older ages (i.e. net consumers) superficially appears unsustainable. For a metric relating the total number of consumers to producers, one can take the population at each age group and weighting by average labour income and consumption at that age.

Technical debate about these different metrics should not obscure the fact that they, and the concept of dependency itself, are political constructs, developed for identifiable political reasons (such as justifying old-age pensions, Winant, 2021) and used for other political reasons (such as the political call for reduced old-age expenditures under the guise of "intergenerational accounting," Cooper, 2021). Statistics are costly to produce which means they are always political (Greer, 2019).

Overall, this chapter has demonstrated that while policy and political debates often talk about older people as if they were a single homogeneous group, in reality what it means to be an older person differs substantially both across countries and within countries. This has important implications, both for how we perceive people at older ages as well as how we should approach policy development in different country settings when it comes to ageing-related policies.

3 | Ageing Equally: Politics, Health and Solidarity

Older people are not a homogeneous social group. Their needs and abilities, and the costs associated with providing for their well-being, vary with their socioeconomic status, gender, geographic location and health status, among other relevant dimensions of difference. It should come as no surprise, then, that older adults are not a politically homogeneous bloc, either. In public and policy conversations there is very often a tendency, however, to assume that older people are a singular pressure group that will act through the political system to secure a distribution of societal resources that primarily benefits them – as retirees, health care consumers, people without young children in the house, and the like. If governments fail to invest in policies that can promote well-being across the life-course, and instead focus on maintaining social expenditure on the current generation of older people by squeezing current workers/future retirees, the story goes, it is because most governments are subject to greater pressure from older voters than from younger citizens, because the former vote at higher rates and are represented by powerful lobby groups. This argument was memorably summarized by the late British journalist Henry Fairlie, writing in *The New Republic* in 1988, as a problem of 'greedy geezers' living well at the expense of the young (Fairlie, 1988).

This chapter evaluates the argument that governments implement packages of policies that are favourable to older people, but that are societally sub-optimal, because of political pressure from older voters. It begins by laying out the core premises of the 'greedy geezer' narrative: because pension transfers, high-cost medical care and policies that protect transferable assets like housing are highly salient to older people and to their advocates, intense preferences for these types of policies communicated to politicians and policymakers will eventually crowd out other, more societally optimal policies. Examples of this narrative in national-level political debates in the UK, Germany, Italy and the USA are presented alongside evidence that many international organizations have also largely accepted the narrative's premises. The chapter next evaluates empirical evidence for and against the core claims of this narrative, drawn mainly from Western European countries where roughly similar party systems and policymaking environments have allowed for systematic analysis that transcends individual country and party cases. Weighing this evidence, the chapter concludes that older people and their organized representatives (e.g. pensioner parties, pensioner unions and advocacy groups) in some contexts do push for policies that are 'greedy' in the sense of being beneficial for older voters and/or their own children, but not for society as a whole. However, this phenomenon is far from universal: it is especially pronounced in the USA and the UK, but much less so in other national contexts.

The chapter goes on to demonstrate that the policy packages adopted by national governments are generally motivated by concerns other than appeasing older voters. Our core argument is that governments do not implement packages of policies that are favourable to older people but societally sub-optimal (because they lead to under-investment in younger people, health inequalities and higher health care spending) *as a result of* pressure from ageing voters and their organized representatives. This is an attribution error – albeit an understandable one, given that many scholars as well as policymakers and members of the public mistakenly assume that social policy choices result primarily from demands from the electorate. But several core features of democratic politics explain why this presumption is incorrect: most people don't usually vote in their own interests; there is a difference between voting for parties and voting for policies; parties say one thing as marketing but often propose policies that are quite different; and parties' manifesto promises are often different from what they actually do. The chapter concludes by arguing that characterizing older people as uniformly 'greedy' obscures the fact that inequality among older adults means that many need more support than they actually receive – a point that we take up in much greater detail later in this volume.

3.1 The 'Greedy Geezer' Narrative

The idea that older voters are responsible for imbalances in social spending priorities that benefit mainly current retirees is itself, well, old. While Fairlie's 1988 *New Republic* article introduced the phrase 'greedy geezers' to the English-speaking world's punditry, scholars had been making more sober claims about the influence of older people on social policy since the mid-1970s. In one of the first cross-national analyses of social spending in OECD countries in 1975, for example, University of California Professor Harold Wilensky argued that increasing allocation of social resources to older adults was a result of ageing populations that created not only a need for more welfare spending (mainly in the form of pensions), but also a political constituency to fight for that spending (Wilensky, 1975). The 1980s saw the development of similar arguments by other welfare state scholars: Pampel and Williamson (1989) found that in democratic countries the 'political pressure of a large aged population' was an important influence on spending; and Thomson (1989) posited the ageing of a politically powerful 'welfare generation' as the driving force behind the growing emphasis of welfare states on programmes for older people versus programmes for children from the 1970s onward. (Thomson would go on to assert more polemically that the 'selfish generation' that reached adulthood just after the Second World War had tailored welfare state spending for its own purposes, and at the expense of the young (Thomson, 1993).)

Whether older people desire social programmes that benefit them directly, or because they want to protect their assets in order to pass them down to their children, the 'greedy geezer' narrative posits that welfare policy mixes emphasizing win-lose solutions – short-term benefits for older people at the expense of longer-term social investment – come about because of political pressure from older voters. Clements (2018) describes such a narrative in the UK, a country where rhetoric blaming older people has been particularly harsh: 'Whether it's the nasty sentiment that Brexit voters are a bunch of selfish old bigots whose demise can't come too soon, or that Baby Boomers have been piling up problems for moaning Millennials, or that old people are just getting in the way with their "bed-blocking" and their unreasonable expectation that younger folk should subsidise their state pensions, free bus passes, TV licences and winter fuel allowances – again and again, we see generational disdain for older people' (Clements, 2018). But even in other countries where the age cleavage is less politicized, similar public pronouncements are common. For example, a 2013 opinion piece in the *Washington Post* titled 'Payments to our elders are harming our future' (Holzer & Sawhill, 2013) was part of 'A meme that has been bubbling up in the media for months' and that 'goes something like this: The elderly have it too good. They claim too much of the country's financial resources and will eat their children's—and grandchildren's—breakfast, lunch, and dinner unless Social Security and Medicare are cut. The country can no longer afford to give seniors so much' (Lieberman, 2013). In Germany, meanwhile, recent reporting claims that 'the data shows that young people feel they've been saddled with the problems of their parents and grandparents – and that their political future has been determined by an older generation [...] "The politics we have now here in Germany are more for middle-aged people, Baby Boomers – not for the younger generation," said Aaron Hinze, a 24-year-old working in health care in Berlin' (Schultheis, 2018).

Midway between politics and scholarship, international organizations have themselves both bought into and promoted the 'greedy geezer' narrative, albeit more subtly. While older adults themselves are generally not blamed explicitly for hijacking the welfare state, population ageing is portrayed as a cataclysmic event for society because of the presumed-inevitable drain that ageing must place on social systems. The World Bank's landmark 1994 report on pension policy, for example – a report that would go on to inform the Bank's pension policy proposals for Eastern Europe and much of the developing world – was titled 'Averting the Old Age Crisis' (World Bank, 1994). The 'crisis' of demographic change, according to the report's Foreword, 'threatens not only the old but also their children and grandchildren, who must shoulder, directly or indirectly, much of the increasingly heavy burden of providing for the aged' (World Bank, 1994, xiii). If this framing seems like a relic of the first, panicky decades in which population ageing emerged as a policy issue, though, consider that the International Monetary Fund stated in their 2004 *World Economic Outlook*, focused on demographic change, contained the caption 'The last train for pension reform leaves in ...' above a figure showing the year at which older voters would surpass 50 per cent of the electorate (IMF, 2004, 165). As recently as 2017, the OECD warned that 'In order to implement the needed reforms popular and political support is needed. Cutting benefits, increasing contributions or raising the retirement age, however, are unpopular. Given the significant political clout of older age groups, pension reforms that limit benefits paid over longer periods might be difficult to pass' (OECD, 2017, 17).

European-level intergovernmental organizations, too, have adopted this narrative. For example, in 2009 the European Commission's Directorate General of Employment, Social Affairs and Equal

Opportunities requisitioned a Flash Eurobarometer poll on intergenerational solidarity. The poll prompted respondents to consider a variety of 'greedy geezer' tropes, including 'Young people and older people do not easily agree on what is best for society', 'Because there will be a higher number of voters decision makers will pay less attention to young people's needs', and 'Older people are a burden for society' (Gallup Organisation, 2009). While the Commission's intention was surely not to stoke intergenerational conflict, the fact that they were concerned enough to ask these questions in a public opinion poll suggests that their own framing of the issue of demographic change was influenced by a narrative that emphasizes the potential for intergenerational conflict resulting from the excessive demands of older adults.

What is the logic underlying the 'greedy geezers' narrative? We can think about social policy priorities, like other goods, as being produced following an interaction between demand and supply. In this case, demand for policies comes from voters and organized interests, while the supply-side of the equation stems from politicians' desires to gain or remain in office. The 'greedy geezers' narrative starts with a demand-side assumption that social policies such as pensions, medical care and policies that protect transferable assets like housing and financial wealth are so salient to older people and their advocates that they tend to crowd out other social policy preferences that might exist in the electorate. If this assumption is correct, then we would expect to see differences in public opinion and political mobilization between older and younger voters when it comes to key social and economic policy issues. We would expect older people to support policies that are in their immediate interest, and not in the interests of younger people. Organized interests acting on behalf of retirees – for example, pensioners' unions, pensioner parties or lobby groups representing seniors – would also be expected to advocate for win-lose policies that protect the immediate financial interests of current elders, including protecting their assets so that they can be passed down to their descendants.

The supply of policies, in this logic, depends on politicians being exquisitely sensitive to the perceived electoral power of older voters. Politicians may themselves be indifferent about whether win-win or win-lose policies are best, but they cater to the wishes of older people because the latter vote at higher rates than the young and/or because senior lobbies are perceived to pose a threat if angered. The notion of old-age Social Security pensions constituting the 'third rail' of American politics – 'touch it, you're dead', electorally – exemplifies this aspect of the 'greedy geezers' narrative[1]. If this assumption is correct, we would expect to see parties with more older voters advocating more win-lose policies; evidence that political parties, candidates and ministers make win-lose policies in response to perceived pressure from older voters; and politicians seeking to minimize the visibility of their actions to older voters when they must go against their preferences.

The 'greedy geezer' narrative draws on some objective political realities, but it ignores others. As a result, it is partly correct, but also misleading. The remainder of this chapter demonstrates this by drawing on the recent published empirical work in political science. It is true that as populations age, older voters make up a larger share of the electorate, and many of them do place a higher priority on some policies that will benefit older people. In some cases, this may lead to sacrificing some policies that will benefit younger people. However, older voters also hold many policy preferences that are similar to those of younger people. Moreover, older people do not tend to vote as a bloc or to mobilize politically on behalf of win-lose policy issues that benefit them alone. These findings from recent political science research cast doubt on the demand-driven explanation for policymakers' tendency to enact win-lose rather than win-win policies. Factors affecting the supply side – for example, the structure of politics and policymaking, and the preferences of other actors such as politicians and peak organizations of business and labour – play a much larger role than the demographics of the electorate in determining the policy mix pursued by governments.

3.2 The Demand-Side Explanation for Win-Lose Policies: Partially, but Only Partially, Correct

The 'greedy geezer' narrative rests on two assumptions: that older people are likely to prefer win-lose social spending on generous pensions and medical care over the expansion of benefits such as education, child care or preventive health; and that when older people make up a large share of the electorate and have strong organized interests working on

---

[1] The metaphor is usually attributed to former Speaker of the US House of Representatives, Thomas P. 'Tip' O'Neill, who is said to have used it in the context of debates over the reform of Social Security pensions. However, it seems likely that the phrase originated with his aide, Kirk O'Donnell (Safire, 2007)).

their behalf, their policy preferences will tend to dominate those of the young. While much of the received wisdom on the political challenges of ageing populations, particularly connected to the welfare state, begins with these assumptions, empirical scholarship on public opinion and voting behaviour offers only partial support for them.

3.2.1 Older People Do Make Up a Large Share of Voters

Older people are indeed a growing share of the electorate, both because of their increasing share in the population, and because they have a higher propensity to vote than do younger age groups (Figure 3.1). In most European countries the share of adults who report having voted in the previous election rises with age until around age 70 (Bussolo et al., 2015, 265). In some countries a combination of local demographic conditions, voting behaviour and first-past-the-post electoral systems make the older share of the electorate seem particularly relevant. For example, in the 2010 UK general election, half of the constituencies in England, Scotland and Wales had electorates in which voters aged 55 and up constituted a majority (Chaney, 2013, 458)[2].

The reasons why older people vote at higher rates than younger people may be related strictly to age: by virtue of having spent more of their lives at or above the voting age, older people may be more strongly habituated to voting (Goerres, 2007). However, high voting rates among older adults may also be a result of period or cohort effects: today's older people have a stronger normative attachment to voting because of their political socialization in the immediate post-war period (Goerres, 2007), while post-Baby Boom generations vote at lower rates than earlier cohorts (Bhatti & Hansen, 2012, 271). If very high voting rates are unique to people socialized in the immediate post-war period, differences in turnout rates between age groups may well decline in future elections. Such an outcome is predicted for Germany (Konzelmann et al., 2012, 259), although empirical analysis for many other countries is not available.

---

[2] It is worth noting, however, that turnout among younger voters has risen in many contexts in very recent years. For example, in the 2019 European Parliament elections turnout among the eligible population aged 16–24 years increased by 14 percentage points compared to 2014, and among 25 to 39 year olds, the increase was 12 per cent. Meanwhile, turnout among eligible voters aged 55+ increased by only 3 per cent.

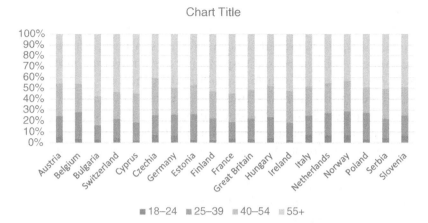

Figure 3.1 Share of the electorate in the last national election by age group, European countries.

Source: European Social Survey Round 9, 2018

3.2.2 Sometimes Older Adults Prefer Win-Lose Policies, and Act Politically to Try to Get Them

If older people are likely to rise as a share of the electorate, at least in the near term, it may be that politicians will be inclined to pay particular attention to their interests. There is a correlation between the share of older people in the population and among voters (Krieger et al., 2013; Sanz & Velázquez, 2007; Shelton, 2008; Tepe & Vanhuysse, 2010). But one cannot conclude from this that social spending priorities are the outcome of political pressure from older voters. One reason is that to a certain extent, pension spending is mechanically related to population ageing: as long as the average benefit level remains constant or rises, more beneficiaries will mean more aggregate spending. Moreover, if the budget for total social spending is fixed or shrinking, increased pension spending will translate into less spending on other kinds of social benefits, including education and child benefits. Thus, a higher share of spending on older people is very likely to occur in ageing populations even without any political pressure from older voters.

This implies that in order to confirm the 'greedy geezer' narrative that policies favouring older people result from demand from an ageing and selfish electorate, we must at the very least show that older voters and lobby groups want and demand something different from younger voters and the organized interests that represent them. What does the best available evidence tell us in this regard? Several studies of age-based social policy preferences in Europe have found that older adults or retired respondents are on average more supportive of increasing pension spending than they are of increasing public education spending (Busemeyer et al., 2009; Mello et al., 2017; Sørensen, 2013). One study also finds that Swiss people over age 50 are four percentage points more likely than people aged 30–49 to prioritize health spending over education spending (Cattaneo & Wolter, 2009, 234).

Moreover, there is some evidence that on average older people do not only hold different social policy preferences than younger people, but also vote on the basis of those preferences. It can be difficult to tell why voters in different age groups vote for particular parties or candidates, and hence hard to assess whether voters are expressing their policy preferences (rather than for example their preferences on other issues, their long-term partisan affiliations or their general ideological orientations) when they vote. However, a study of voting patterns in Swiss referenda on specific social policy initiatives between 1981 and 2004 found that even after controlling for ideology, 'Older generations not only massively approve[d] improvements in the benefits they receive, but they also tend[ed] to reject social policy proposals aimed at improving the situation of the actively employed and of young families' (Bonoli & Häusermann, 2009, 13). While voting for pensioner parties is rare – pensioner parties have had very little success in most European countries (Hanley, 2010, 2013) – support for pensioner parties may also be interpreted as being linked to policy preferences favouring retirees. One study found that Dutch pensioner parties have captured voters who wish to advance their relatively well-protected position in the welfare state (Otjes & Krouwel, 2018, 41–2).

Beyond voting, the interests of the seniors may be represented outside of the electoral arena by pensioners' unions and advocacy groups. While few advocacy groups for older people in Europe have the political clout of the Association for the Advancement of Retired Persons (AARP) in the USA, organizations working on behalf of older adults and retirees can have an important role in policy, especially where pensioners' unions or civil society groups are incorporated into the policy process via neo-corporatist or other consultation processes (see Anderson & Lynch, 2007; Campbell & Lynch, 2000; Chiarini, 1999; Lambelet, 2011).

3.2.3 Social Policy Preferences of Older and Younger People Are Often Not As Different As We Expect

While on some issues and in some countries some older voters may prefer different policies than do younger ones, the most recent large-scale survey of social policy preferences reveals a complex relationship between age, retirement and social policy preferences once political ideology and other potential confounds are controlled for. Instead of the predicted cleavage in social policy preferences, Garritzmann et al. (2018) find that across eight Western European countries retirees, like younger people, strongly support social investment policies such as early childhood education, job training and higher education spending, while they oppose more generous passive transfers such as pensions, early retirement and unemployment benefits. In this study, the exceptional group preferring more generous passive transfers is people aged 50–59, not retirees. This study echoes the abundant literature on social policy preferences that finds that age, cohort or retirement status per se generally have very little, if any, predictive power above and beyond left-right political ideology, gender, country of residence, etc. (see Busemeyer et al., 2018; Busemeyer et al., 2008; Goerres & Tepe, 2010; Kohli, 2015; Komp, 2013; Krieger et al., 2013; Lynch & Myrskylä, 2009; Mello et al., 2017; Sørensen, 2013; Walczak et al., 2012).

One reason for the consistent finding of only minor differences in social policy preferences according to age is that 'older people' are in reality a diverse group. Older voters differ from the young in terms of their political socialization and their personal ideologies and preferences (on average today's older adults are somewhat further to the left on most economic and welfare policies than are the young or middle-aged (Caughey et al., 2019; Ferguson & de Weck, 2019)), but they also differ amongst themselves in ways that are likely to affect their policy preferences. Age (young-old versus old-old), class and the specific features of the social, economic and policy context in different countries have all been found to predict important differences in social policy preferences among older voters (Busemeyer et al., 2008; Fairlie, 1988; Fernández & Jaime-Castillo, 2013; Goerres & Vanhuysse, 2012; Komp & van Tilburg, 2010; Naumann, 2014; Sabbagh & Vanhuysse, 2010; Tosun et al., 2012; Vidovičová & Honelová, 2018). These findings are, of course, consistent with core findings of the broader political science literature that (a) many demographic characteristics are strongly associated with public opinions and political behaviours, and (b) existing institutions and policies have an independent effect on opinions and behaviours.

3.3 Older Voters Do Not Vote As a Bloc

Age is associated with patterns of voting for one party versus another in many European party systems, as well as at the European level. For example, exit polling during the 2019 European Parliament elections showed that as compared to voters under the age of 35, older voters were markedly less likely to vote for a Green Party candidate and more likely to vote for a centre-right (EPP) or conservative (ECR) candidate (see Figure 3.2).

However, belonging to the category of 'the elderly' does not generally translate into distinctive voting patterns once one takes into account the sociodemographic factors that are associated with both age and party choice. Analysis of European Social Survey data shows that after controlling for factors such as gender, household income, social class, religiosity, rural residence and ideological orientation, it is possible to predict party choice based on belonging to the 55+ age group for only a

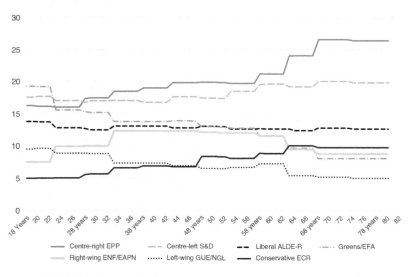

Figure 3.2 Vote shares of party groups by age, 2019 European Parliament elections.

Source: Figure produced with data provided by Tobias Schminke, based on Schminke (2019).

small number of cases of parties in Europe – fewer parties, in fact, than would be predicted by chance alone (see the Appendix to this chapter for details of the analysis). The fact that some of the very few parties that do receive disproportionate support from older voters – for example the Conservative Party in the UK – are unusually prominent in the minds of English-speaking analysts likely drives a perception that membership of the 'elderly' age group matters more than it actually does for voting.

Even in those cases where differential voting by age group does occur, it is not always clear that the consolidation of support among older voters has an effect on the policy outputs of governments. This is a consequence of the demographic diversity of older people: while they may form a large voting group, they do not necessarily act *as a group*, and hence may have difficulty translating even those policy preferences that they share into effective political pressure. As Goerres (2008) explains, 'A political cleavage is a line of conflict along which parties mobilize their constituents, meaning that that conflict becomes politically decisive. There are three stages in the development of a cleavage: (1) social groups can differentiate among each other by a set of social characteristics that are somehow socially constructed and accepted; (2) political parties exist that use these social features to frame their messages; (3) voters of a given social group use their own social definition as a shortcut to vote for the party representing their group, thereby politically reinforcing the division line. If age were a political cleavage, we would need to see at least one party popular among the old and another party popular among the young.' Yet this differential partisan mobilization by age is unlikely in many contexts both because parties (and unions) have traditionally managed the demands of multiple generations (Kohli, 1999), and because older voters are generally among the least likely to switch their institutional affiliations (Goerres, 2009). As of 2003, even in the USA and the UK, where the age cleavage was relatively strongly represented by advocacy organizations not linked to parties, voters did 'not tend to vote as an interest group' (Vincent, 2003, 10).

The period since 2010, which has witnessed much greater electoral volatility in Europe, presents an opportunity for a realignment of party systems around an age cleavage, but it is too soon to tell if that has happened. Even if parties were to focus on an age cleavage, which is unlikely, an age cleavage is unlikely to have the permanence of other cleavages such as race, ethnicity or class, for the simple reason that we all age. Parties may try to build coalitions around age for a decade or two, but today's older voters will not be around for much more than that, and in a decade or two middle-aged voters will be older themselves. Nationality, race and class reproduce across generations; generations obviously cannot.

If mainstream parties have not reorganized around an age cleavage, neither have pensioner parties successfully replaced them as representatives of older voters. Pensioner parties have emerged in several European countries but have gained parliamentary representation in only two (the Netherlands and Luxembourg) and are generally negligible political forces (Bussolo et al., 2015; Gilleard & Higgs, 2009; Goerres, 2008; Hanley, 2010). Nor have the older people influenced policy as a bloc through other modes of political participation beyond voting. While nonconventional forms of participation like protesting, demonstrating and petitioning are rising in younger age groups (Albacete, 2014; Tiberj, 2017), older adults are significantly less active than young or middle-aged people when it comes to non-electoral forms of participation (Goerres & Tepe, 2010; Melo & Stockemer, 2014, 45–6). Senior advocacy groups can be effective mouthpieces for the interests of older people as a bloc, but even when large these groups are not always effective (Goerres [2008] notes that the VDK Deutschland, an older persons' interest organization with 1.4 million members, has had little influence on policy). And Campbell and Lynch (2000) find that very large, powerful interest groups like the AARP and Italian pensioners' unions have professionalized staffs that are often motivated to moderate the demands of pensioners in order to ensure the long-term sustainability of the welfare state, blunting the potential impact of 'greedy geezers' on policy demands.

If older people hold policy preferences that are often indistinguishable from those of younger voters, if they have not aligned themselves with mainstream parties in order to function as a voting bloc, and if their organized representatives are either impotent or disinclined to pursue a win-lose policy strategy of increasing benefits for seniors at the expense of social investment, then it should not come as a surprise that 'the elderly are not successful in setting a political agenda. They do not influence the party manifestos, the electoral debate [...]. Compared to groups who are much smaller, for example the farmers, gun owners, or policemen, they are relatively ineffective. And even taking into account their difficulties of physical mobility and resources, older people do not mobilise militant support in the manner of road protesters, animal rights, or disabled activists. While pensioners organisations are able to hold mass meetings, marches and lobbies they do not attract the attention or the political clout that the numbers of older people in the community suggest they might' (Vincent, 2003, 10).

3.4 The Supply-Side Explanation for Win-Lose Policies Is Also Partly, but Only Partly, Right

The logic of the 'greedy geezers' narrative, in addition to resting on a partially incorrect assumption that older people hold social policy preferences that are distinct from the young and vote in a bloc to express those preferences, requires that politicians supply the policies that they do in response to pressure from older voters or interest groups. In this essentially pluralist and representational logic, policymakers respond to external pressures from competing groups in the electorate, and *only* to those external pressures. Decades of political science research on the welfare state and policymaking have shown that this model, while compelling as a heuristic, does not capture the full range of influences on policy outputs, many of which come from the supply side rather than the demand side of politics. This section first examines evidence for the responsiveness of politicians to pressure from groups of older people in the electorate, and then explores other influences that might affect the supply of win-win vs. win-lose social policies.

3.4.1 There Is Some Evidence of Politicians Responding to Demands from Older Voters When Making Social Policy Choices

If older people make up a large group in the electorate, are not locked in to voting for a particular party and have distinctive policy preferences, then we can expect politicians to supply policies that appeal to this group in an effort to court their votes. The UK offers an example of this dynamic: Chaney's analysis of election manifestos in the UK during the post-war period revealed an increase in the salience and detail of policies directed at older adults. But it is not clear how widespread this pattern is across European democracies (Chaney, 2013). It is possible that the first-past-the-post electoral system and a high concentration of older voters in particular districts in recent decades make the UK an unusual case, and there have been few empirical studies of the responsiveness of parties or politicians to seniors.

One area in which parties and politicians are often presumed to be quite sensitive to the preferences of older voters is in the area of pension reform, and narrative accounts of pension reform often include references to a 'backlash from pensioners' (Wisensale, 2013, 25), governments fearing to 'ace their electorates' (Casey, 2012, 260), or unspecified 'electoral pressures' (Weaver & Torp, 2015, 76). Indeed, Pierson's 'new politics' theory (Pierson, 1994, 1996) predicts that the politics of contemporary social policy will be marked by a distinct age dimension. According to Pierson, politicians seek to claim credit for expanding social benefits, and to avoid blame for withdrawing them. In the context of mature welfare states, the limited scope for expansion is mainly to cover previously excluded groups and 'new social risks' (Armingeon & Bonoli, 2007) that have emerged with the breakdown of lifetime employment and the male-breadwinner family model – most of which could be categorized as win-win policy, and much of which is aimed at children and working-age people. Meanwhile, the targets of contraction in mature welfare states are likely to be the beneficiaries of large, well-established, expensive social programmes whose costs are driven even higher by population ageing: pensions and medical care. The 'new politics' of the welfare state, then, can be expected to have an age dimension: when politicians seek to claim credit for expanding social benefits, it should be with younger voters, and their primary relationship with older voters should be one of blame avoidance.

However, more recent empirical literature on blame avoidance generally finds limited support for the most simplistic formulations of the theory that posit a direct relationship between policy proposals and perceived electoral pressure. Indeed, in their comprehensive study of pension politics in Western European countries, Immergut and Anderson (2009) find only rare instances – for example in the Netherlands – where the electoral system, the distribution of the electorate and the structure of the pension system combine to make politicians keenly sensitive to electoral pressures from the older voters.

3.4.2 Policy Is Mainly a Response to Factors Other Than Pressure from Older People

In far more country cases, Immergut and Anderson (2009) found, politicians were motivated in their pension reform attempts by their ideological beliefs about social programmes (Schumacher et al., 2013,

17); by their perception of the need for immediate system change; by the demands of unions, whose social policy preferences were more or less friendly to current retirees depending on their role in managing the pension system and/or on their organizational structure; by pressure from specific groups of current or retired workers, such as farmers or public sector employees, who enjoyed special pension privileges; by influence from international organizations like the OECD, World Bank, IMF or European monetary regulators; and by powerful financial market actors with a stake in pension system organization (see also Naczyk, 2013). In other words, pension policy resulted from a complex mix of politicians seeking to avoid blame or claim credit from numerous constituencies.

Another reason why older voters do not drive an agenda tailored to 'greedy geezers' is that in most polities, policy is only partially a product of electoral demands. The institutional landscape presented by electoral and governance systems also has an important impact on social policy-making. The Swiss system, with its frequent recourse to policymaking by referendum, is very likely an outlier. But even there a recent study found that on average the policy preferences of parliamentarians were closest to those of the young and furthest from those of older voters (Kissau et al., 2012, 74–5). And ministries and their staffs are generally even further removed than are parliaments from the pressures of the electorate. In countries where inclusion of the social partners and/or civil society groups in policymaking is customary, the preferences of atomized voters may have even less of an impact on legislation.

Where electoral politics does matter for social policymaking, it is very often not in the form of a simple equilibrium balancing demand from voters with supply of policy solutions by politicians. Instead, just as in health care, the providers (in this case politicians) often over-supply particular goods in response to other incentives. Lynch (2006) showed that the dominant mode of political competition (particularistic or programmatic) in a country, rather than electoral pressure from senior or youth organizations, determined politicians' choices about how to structure social policies, and that these choices in turn resulted in different age-orientations of social spending in OECD countries as populations aged. Similarly, Immergut and Anderson (2009) found that expansion or contraction of pension entitlements in Western European countries depends in part on the intensity of political competition, which is determined by a combination of the electoral system, the party system and whether the geographic distribution of preferences in the electorate aligns with districts in a way that provokes politician responsiveness.

The contemporary politics of social policy is also determined to a very large extent by actual or perceived fiscal constraints. A combination of pressures from population, low employment and the Maastricht Treaty (which formalized debt and deficit criteria for entry into the EMU in 1992) prompted strong efforts at budgetary control in many continental European governments, which affected social policy programmes as well as other areas of public spending. In some instances, as in Italy, the Netherlands, Germany, and France, this contributed in the 1990s and 2000s to tipping the balance of social spending somewhat away from passive social policies benefiting primarily older workers and future retirees, and towards a greater emphasis on benefits for the young, such as cash transfers for lone parents, early childhood education and job training for unemployed youth. Pressures for budgetary restraint also encouraged some governments in the higher-spending continental social-insurance-based systems to seek cost savings in health care. These efforts affected health care users by increasing out-of-pocket payments (often exempting older people and those with low incomes, however) and, in some instances, diverting health sector resources to less costly preventive services and health promotion. On balance, fiscal pressures, at least in continental Europe and prior to the crisis, may have stimulated a politics of turning 'vice into virtue' (Levy, 1999) that resulted in a recalibration of social policy systems to include more win-win policies. Budgetary politics since the global financial and Eurozone crises, however, have resulted (especially in Southern Europe) in more indiscriminate cuts to social services and health systems that are likely to have a more negative impact on younger people.

3.5 Weighing the Evidence

3.5.1 Are Older People 'Greedy', Rationally Demanding, or Deserving?

On some issues, and in some contexts, older adults do mobilize politically in defence of their interests as older people and in order to protect their assets or income. But there is considerable variation across both issues and contexts. In terms of contexts, it seems to be in the UK and the USA that the most pronounced generational or age cleavage appears in support for a range of issues from school funding to housing policy to pensions (see e.g. Lynch & Myrskylä, 2009 on pension income as a determinant of preferences in the UK as compared to other European countries). This may be related to the fact that these liberal welfare states provide fewer protections for their citizens overall. A scarcity of social resources may lead older people to be more assertive in protecting the transfer payments on which they rely and the assets that they have accumulated and that may be an important source of financial security for them and their children.

Some issue areas may also be more apt than others to generate age-based differences of opinion and political mobilization. I have examined age-based attitudes mainly in the arena of income transfers and social services, and in these domains older people have often been protected from immediate cutbacks by 'grandfather' clauses or age-based exemptions from user fees, even as younger people also continue to enjoy access to benefits. It is perhaps not surprising, then, that there is broad societal consensus on the desirability of continued state provision of many forms of transfers and services. However, when asset-based welfare supplants direct provision of social benefits, older people may develop sharper interests in taxing, zoning, financial regulation and other policies that protect accumulated wealth. To the extent that older people have lived through periods where there were opportunities for asset accumulation while younger people have not, their preferences may on average diverge. Even so, under these circumstances some younger adults may have a shared interest in policies that protect the assets of their parents, which they may expect to inherit.

The interests that older people have in policies that protect their incomes and/or assets may be rationally demanding, rather than unreasonable or greedy, to the extent that they are needed to ensure their wellbeing in the context of broader social policy arrangements. Indeed, such policy preferences may be supported by society at large if they are perceived as necessary for ensuring an equitable distribution of resources to a group that might otherwise be poor. Policies favouring older adults may also be supported by social narratives that cast older people as especially 'deserving' because of their past contributions to overall economic development and/or social insurance programmes, or because of their status as respected elders. These social narratives might even help to explain how governments could produce a win-lose policy mix: if working-aged adults (and their children) are seen as especially undeserving of social support relative to older people, investments in early stages of the life-course may be crowded out by policies that benefit mainly current seniors.

3.5.2 Social Policies Generally Result Mainly from Considerations Unrelated to Demand from Voters

While it is tempting to assume that in representative democracies demand from (different groups in) the electorate explains whether politicians and policymakers provide win-win versus win-lose policy mixes, the supply of policies is in fact very often due to other factors. Decades of research into patterns of social policy provision have highlighted several factors as particularly relevant to the supply of win-win policy.

Policy drift results when politicians and policymakers fail to update policies to keep up with larger social, demographic or economic changes that affect the outputs of policies (Hacker, 2004). Lynch (2001, 2006) found that the age-orientation of social spending in OECD countries is due not to politicians responding in real time to demands from the electorate, but rather to politicians' differential propensity to update social welfare systems to compensate for demographic trends in political systems characterized by different types of political competition.

Provider groups can also be an important source of political pressure for social policies whose interests may either diverge from or amplify the voices of the consumers of social policy. For example, Giaimo (2002) highlights the role of doctors and Perera (2018, 2019) the role of public sector social service providers in demanding expanded service provision; and Naczyk (2013) and Anderson (2019) show how the financialization of pension systems in recent years has led to a growing influence of financial market actors on pension policymaking.

A commitment to *evidence-based policymaking* can provide a pathway for scientific research to influence policy, especially when there is a strong consensus in the research community about the costs and benefits of certain policy approaches. As we outline in Chapter 2, there is abundant evidence of the benefits of win-win policies for population health, equity and financial sustainability. However, institutional, professional and political barriers can stand in the way of evidence being taken up in policy, and may help to explain variation in the passage or implementation of policies that are widely believed to be promising (Smith, 2007, 2013).

Pressure from *international actors* – from bond traders to the European Commission to the World Health Organization – can also affect the behaviour of domestic policymakers. Financial market actors and European regulators may exert pressure to constrain the growth of public spending (Mosley, 2000) and/or open up markets for financial and other services to international competition (Greer et al., 2019; Koivusalo, 2014). The EU, WHO and other international organizations may also play a role in stimulating policy development through soft law mechanisms such as the open method of coordination (Barcevicius & Weishaupt, 2014) or policy initiatives like Health For All (Lynch, 2020).

Finally, in the current political and economic environment, *fiscal constraints* may be the most important determinant of social policy development. Whether acting through bond market yields, imposed from above during European Semester negotiations, and/or undertaken voluntarily by domestic party-political actors, the rhetoric and practice of austerity shape the possibilities open for policymakers to pursue investments in human capital across the life-course.

3.6 Conclusion

This chapter has shown that the narrative of the 'greedy geezer' or 'selfish generation' imposing their political will and preventing investments in win-win social policies is largely a figment of our collective imagination. There are circumstances in which older voters may act 'selfishly' on behalf of their children, for example by seeking to protect their investments in housing that they plan to pass down to future generations, and too rigidly restricting redistribution to within families, rather than across them to support the neediest, is deleterious not only for health but for social justice. Even so, there is considerable space for demands from older voters that would be socially desirable. Not only the most deprived elderly (who cannot rightly be called 'greedy' if they ask for more than they are getting), but all those who stand to benefit from policies that promote healthy and active ageing should be encouraged to advocate for these policies that benefit the whole of society.

3.7 Appendix

For the analysis of the distinctiveness of elderly support for particular parties we estimated a series of binomial logit models for each European party, country and year (wave) in the most recent two full waves of the ESS dataset (corresponding to 2014 and 2016). The quantity of interest was the binomial regression coefficient on the age group 55+, which represents the increment in support for a party among that age group as compared to the reference group of people aged 25–39. We selected age 25–39 as the reference category to allow for maximum potential contrast, since those aged 40–54 have been found to have ageing-related policy preferences more similar to those of the 'elderly' (aged 55+). We limited the sample of parties to those receiving at least 5 per cent of the national vote in the election immediately preceding the relevant wave of the survey. We excluded countries in which more than 30 per cent of respondents in any age group (25–39, 40–54, 55+) was missing data on household income, as well as all respondents below the age of 25 (due to a high degree of missingness on income in that age group). Remaining missing data for household income and other variables were multiplied using multivariate imputation by chained equations (mice routine in R) and predictive mean matching method based on all other variables included in the models. Among all respondents from a given country and wave, we predicted the propensity to vote for each party in the system based first on age group alone, and then additionally controlling for age in years, gender, primary education, tertiary education, household income (in deciles of the national income distribution), household income mainly from pensions (including disability, old-age and widow/ers' pensions), religiosity, current or former union membership, living in a rural area, belonging to a group that is discriminated against in the respondent's country, and self-placement on the left-right ideological spectrum. We ran a total of 445 (221 for 2014 and 224 for 2016) fully controlled models on thirty-eight countries (nineteen for each wave), and found a total of sixteen parties (four for 2014 and twelve for 2016) for which belonging to the 55+ age group was a significant positive predictor of voting in the previous national election at the standard .05 per cent confidence level. No party had a significant effect of belonging to the 55+ age group in both 2014 and 2016. The magnitude and significance of the coefficient on the 55+ age group in each party model is reported in Table A1.

4 | *The Coalitional Politics of Win-Wins*

4.1 Introduction

Despite the alleged bias towards older people in many political institutions in Europe, this chapter argues that policymakers often do not introduce the most effective policies for supporting healthy ageing. The following pages show that while public spending on older people (e.g. pensions, old age care) remains more extensive and insulated from cuts than other forms of spending, in many (not all) countries policymakers do not introduce policies that would help people age in a healthy way. These latter policies, which include spending on the poorest older people, ensuring access to high quality services and investing across the life-cycle to enable people to enter old age in good health, are often limited.

The chapter then argues that to understand why political institutions simultaneously seem to cater to the needs of older people while often failing to support healthy ageing, we need to conceptualize how the politics of ageing intersect with class, gender and regional dynamics. Building on the framework from the introduction, the chapter turns to the politics of 'win-win' ageing policies. It argues that where political conflict over policies is framed largely intergenerationally, the wellbeing of older people may be preserved in the short run, but less investment in the long-run infrastructure of healthy ageing emerges. By contrast, where cross-class/cross-generational coalitions come together to address gender and class inequities (among the elderly and working age) and develop public services, win-win models can emerge.

4.1.1 *Intra- and Intergenerational Solidarity Across Europe*

One of the core arguments of this book is that policies can powerfully shape the way that individual people, geographic places and larger polities experience demographic changes. Policies will shape whether older people experience more poverty and insecurity in the future than today, whether they have access to high quality services and how the costs of ageing are distributed. That policies matter for health ageing is obvious, but what policies matter? When, and where, are they likely to occur? Do democratic processes supply the policies that public health scholars identify as central to health ageing? The following pages argue that healthy ageing requires attention to policies well beyond health itself, something that democratic politics can, but often does not, supply.

First, healthy ageing requires attention to both access to health care and inequalities amongst older people – what we label below *intragenerational equality*. One of the key claims developed in this book is that older people are not a homogeneous group, but have different needs, capacities and resources. Where policies compensate for these differences by providing access to public services – and, crucially, reduce poverty and inequality amongst the elderly, they also provide the scope for healthy ageing.

Figure 4.1 gives an example of these dynamics. It shows the average share of elderly adult respondents in the EU-SILC survey in 2015 who reported being in 'very good' or 'good' health (as opposed to 'fair', 'bad'

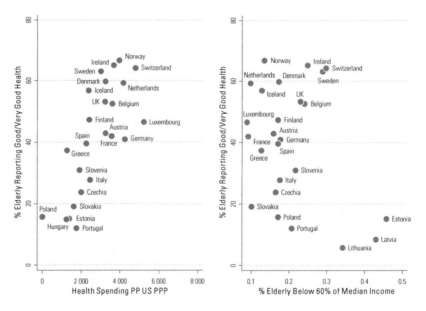

Figure 4.1 Average share of elderly adult respondents.

Source: EU-SILC, 2015

or 'very bad' health) on the y-axis, plotted against health spending on the x-axis in panel a and elderly poverty rates (measured as 60 per cent of median income) on the x-axis in panel b. Descriptively, Figure 4.1 shows that older people in countries with more health care spending tend to report higher levels of health (the country level correlation in 2015 was r=.75). However, countries with more health care spending also tend to be wealthier and have larger welfare states, with Lynch (2020) arguing that actual health is a product of the larger approach to tackling income inequality. Panel b demonstrates this pattern, showing a slightly weaker, but still substantial correlation between post-tax and transfer poverty rates among the elderly and self-reported health.

Second, however, healthy ageing does not start in old age. Attention to the wellbeing of children and working age populations shapes longer-run trajectories. As we argue in Chapters 5 and 6, poverty and low-income during the working years are linked to lower life expectancy and health risks in old age. Financial stress, lack of access to health care and poor nutrition during childhood and the working years impact both the health risks people face as they enter old age and the resources they have to support themselves. Equally, the skills and activities of the non-elderly population provide key economic and social resources to support those who are already in old age. As Anton Hemerijck (2017) powerfully argues, so called 'social investment' policies that support children, families and skill acquisition through the life-cycle are crucial to funding and sustaining more traditional support policies for older people. In other words, *intergenerational equality* also is a critical component of healthy ageing.

Figure 4.2, using OECD data averaged over the five-year 2011–2016 period, shows substantial differences in the degree of solidarity within and across generations. On the x-axis, it shows the percentage of older people whose income is less than 60 per cent of the median income. Under 5 per cent of older people are poor based on this definition in the Netherlands, France and Norway (among others), but close to 30 per cent of older people are poor in Estonia. The y-axis demonstrates the share of working age adults who are poor. In a few cases, like Estonia, more than twice as many older people are poor than working age adults, whereas in the Southern European countries, poverty amongst older people is lower than amongst working age adults. Other countries, like Germany and Austria, take a more intermediate position, with roughly similar rates of poverty among older people and working age adults. In

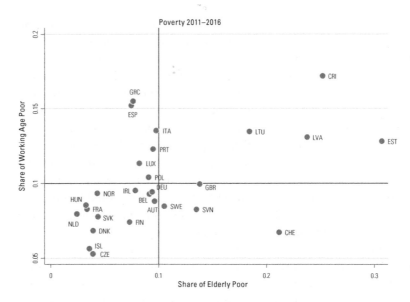

Figure 4.2 Differences in the degree of solidarity within and across generations.

short, there is substantial variation in the degree of intragenerational distribution of resources (i.e. inequality amongst the older and working age cohorts) and the intergenerational distribution of resources (i.e. the relative rates of poverty of older people versus working age adults and children).

Policies shape both intra- and intergenerational solidarity. One of the great public policy successes of the twentieth century was a dramatic reduction of poverty among older people. In the early part of the twentieth century elderly adults, lacking a market income in retirement, were very often poor, relying on their meagre savings or family members to support them, with little additional public or private support. The expansion of public pensions, private occupational pensions and the development of private savings products have allowed people to smooth consumption over their lifetime, dramatically reducing rates of poverty from the early post-war era. However, the extent to which countries adopted these policies varies dramatically. Where welfare policies are more meagre or limited, or ignore the specific risks that some categories of older people face, we may see weaker intragenerational solidarity and more inequality amongst the elderly. By contrast, policies that limit such inequalities are generous pensions, health care systems with limited out-of-pocket payments, and accessible and subsidized care services.

Elsewhere, Julia Lynch (2006) demonstrates how different welfare states target non-health spending across age groups, showing differences in the extent to which welfare states devote resources to welfare *and* target these resources to older people. Where policies are targeted largely at the needs of, or risks faced by, older people, and do not cover those in working age, it can weaken intergenerational solidarity. Conversely, policies that target risks over the life-cycle, including programmes aimed at child poverty (child benefits, housing benefits, in-work benefits or tax credits for families) and childcare, and those for out-of-work adults (both through unemployment and long-run disability), can reduce inequality and poverty among younger people and reduce gaps in both programmatic focus and social outcomes across age groups.

Building on Lynch, we distinguish among four configurations of policy outcomes based on how they redistribute across and within generations. As articulated in earlier chapters, we argue that a win-win configuration pays attention to both inter and intragenerational solidarity. By contrast, a more residual path adopts a more meagre welfare state, accomplishing neither form of solidarity. Age-focused paths are relatively generous for older people, reducing inequality and poverty amongst older people, but do less for working age adults. Finally, some countries offer a limited form of universalism, providing funding across the generations but leaving substantial inequalities in place.

These differences are not merely theoretical, but capture varying choices made across advanced welfare states. Figure 4.3 shows the cross-sectional variation in welfare spending, building on a modified version of Lynch's (2006) original measure, comparing non-health spending that primarily goes to older people to spending that primarily goes to

Table 4.1 *Paths of solidarity*

	High Intergenerational Solidarity	Low Intergenerational Solidarity
High Solidarity Amongst Elderly	Win-Win	Age Focused
Low Solidarity Amongst Elderly	Universal Limited	Residual

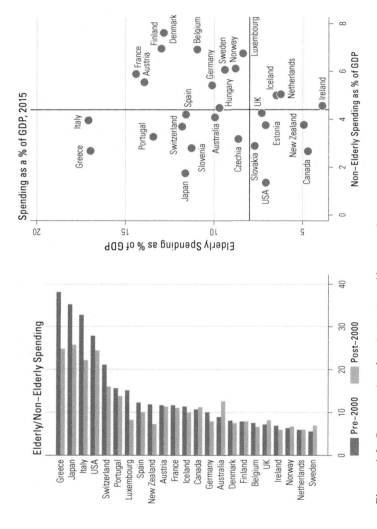

Figure 4.3 Cross-sectional variation in welfare spending.

Source: Building on Lynch, 2006

non-older people (working age adults and children), relative to their population shares[1]. On the left we see the ratio of the two figures, and on the right the unweighted spending data.

These data show, first, that some countries both distribute resources across the full life-cycle and are relatively generous. In other words, they follow a 'win-win' approach. Historically, the Scandinavian countries developed along these lines, establishing generous pensions and other benefits for the elderly next to working age benefits such as unemployment insurance, later extending extensive benefits to children through the expansion of parental leave policies and other forms of 'social investment' (Morel et al., 2012). The policies that produce this path include child benefits and care services for the very young, housing for young families, training and unemployment benefits for the working age, and large and generous pensions and care services for the elderly, financed by extensive taxes. As shown in Figure 4.3 above, the overall spending generosity in countries like Finland, Denmark, Austria and France matters for social outcomes, limiting inequities both across age groups and within age groups.

A second group of countries have more extensive safety nets for older people than for working age adults or children, redistributing resources to this group. Countries falling closer to the 'age focused' type include Southern European countries like Greece and Italy, as well as Japan. The result is relatively robust protection for older people, but larger gaps between the wellbeing of older people and the working age or child population. In these cases, pensions (and often care) benefits are more extensive than those targeted at young families (housing and childcare services) or working age adults (unemployment benefits). Even where the 'headline' benefits for the working age are quite generous, in practice, in these countries, many workers without permanent jobs are excluded from these benefits, putting them at risk of economic precarity.

---

[1] Spending on older people includes old age pensions and survivors' benefits; non-elderly spending includes spending on incapacity excluding disability pensions, family benefits, unemployment benefits and active labour market benefits. As with Lynch, we exclude housing, other social policy benefits and disability pensions because the age orientation cannot be easily ascertained. One exception is Denmark, where unemployment is counted as private 'other' social policy. Private voluntary spending is not included. All spending is baselined against the share of the elderly in the population. Data are drawn from OECD SOCX, and OECD population data. The inclusion of education spending substantially reduces the gap in spending, but is not strictly social policy. It is therefore not included here.

Third, some countries have more limited welfare states, but a less clear age orientation, or in some cases, a pro-youth structure. The UK forms an example of such a 'universal limited' welfare state, with historically relatively moderate pension benefits and unemployment benefits. In the 2000s, during a period of some welfare expansion, the government uprated both pensions and child and housing benefits, reducing poverty for both groups, but leaving large gaps in coverage among the working age (e.g. limited unemployment benefits, little retraining). In contrast to very meagre systems, there are benefits that moderate income shocks across each stage of the life-cycle, but the smaller size of these benefits leaves the elderly vulnerable to greater poverty.

Finally, in a fourth group of countries, solidarity is low both across and within generations, leaving both older people and the working age community exposed. The Eastern European countries in the bottom left quadrant, like Estonia and Slovakia, as well as the USA and Canada, have lower overall spending on both groups, even as the USA is heavily focused on older people overall. The result is higher rates of poverty, and lower solidarity within and across generations.

In sum, Table 4.1 and Figure 4.3 demonstrate that packages of 'win-win' policies exist – and are associated with more equitable outcomes – but they are far from universal. Some countries have developed models of protection that are much more extensively skewed towards older people than other groups, while some provide more meagre benefits overall.

4.2 Intra- and Intergenerational Solidarity in an Era of Austerity

The previous section showed that the variation Lynch (2006) identified in the age-orientation of welfare states, combined with broader and well theorized differences in generosity (e.g. Esping-Andersen, 1990), continue to lead to substantial differences in the way policies shape solidarity across and within generations. However, over the last decades the growth of welfare spending has slowed, overall inequality has risen and substantial cuts in some forms of benefits have occurred, while others have been 'recalibrated' to meet new needs (e.g. Hemerijck, 2013; Huber & Stephens, 2015).

In spite of the promotion of a 'social investment' agenda in the European Union and beyond (Jenson & Saint-Martin, 2003), there has been no uniform trend towards 'win-win' policies. To return to

Figure 4.3, we see substantial overtime continuity. There is some move towards more relative spending on younger people in Southern Europe between 2000 and 2010, but spending on older people in these countries is still more extensive by a wide margin than spending on social benefits for the working age population. The financial crisis of 2008 further unsettled some of these gains for younger people.

Indeed, in the face of more recent fiscal pressures, it appears that the benefits for the elderly have been more robust and less likely to see cuts than benefits for working age adults. Work by Mertens (2017) and Streeck and Mertens (2013) finds that investment spending, including investment in the human capital of the young, has been more vulnerable to cuts than spending on the old in times of fiscal austerity. In the UK, for instance, benefits for working age residents and children have fallen faster than those for the elderly in the post-crisis period.

Figure 4.4 shows these patterns descriptively, demonstrating trends in elderly and working age poverty rates from the late 1990s to the early 2010s, using the Fiscal Redistribution Database, which draws on the Luxembourg Income Study (Wang & Caminada, 2017). Unlike the

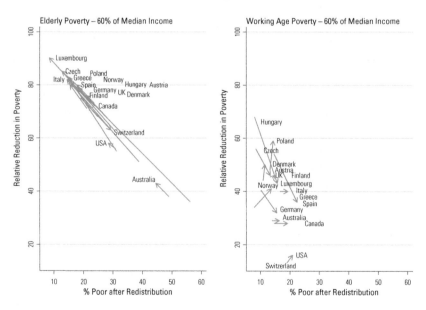

Figure 4.4 Trends in elderly and working age poverty rates from the late 1990s to the early 2010s.

Source: Fiscal Redistribution Database

OECD data above, these data are only available for a smaller range of countries and not for identical periods, but they do exist for a longer time period, allowing an over-time comparison.

Despite some of the limitations of the data, seemingly clear pictures emerge. The x-axis of these graphs, as with Figure 4.2, shows the post-tax and transfer poverty rate for the elderly and working age respectively, with the country labels marking the most recent observation (in the late 2000s or early to mid-2010s). The y-axis shows the relative reduction in poverty from the pre-tax and transfer distribution, in other words, the fiscal effort of the state. What we see is that over time, elderly poverty has fallen in most countries (Switzerland is an exception), while the relative role of redistribution has increased. When we turn to the working age, by contrast, a more diverse set of patterns are at play. In many countries poverty has increased, but in some cases so too has the fiscal effort of the state (e.g. Poland, Norway) while in others the fiscal role of the state has also declined (e.g. Czechia, Germany, Spain).

These trends do not necessarily mean that more age-focused welfare institutions are emerging everywhere. The policy trends are more complex than the outcome data would suggest. First, many cuts to benefits targeted at older people are slow to translate into outcomes, with pension benefit cuts (and expansion) being phased in over many years. Huber and Stephens (2015), in their study of trends in so-called reforms to broad 'social consumption' benefits, argue that a number of cuts to pensions benefits have occurred but that the cuts will become operational in the coming decades. Given uneven private savings and uneven access to private occupational pensions, these shifts portend a long-run reduction in solidarity amongst older people as well as the creation of intergenerational inequities as younger cohorts leave the labour market with less favourable pension arrangements than the older cohorts who were often protected from the immediate consequences of changes in pensions.

Second, for the working age population, in many cases there has been an expansion of transfers to low-income families. A number of countries expanded sometimes quite substantially benefits for families and parental leave through the 1990s and 2000s, including Germany (Morgan, 2013), the UK (Hills et al., 2016) and even parts of Southern Europe. However, at the same time these same countries have cut core income replacement programmes. Rueda (2015) argues, more generally, that existing spending on the working age in areas of unemployment and active labour market programmes constitute less of a buffer against insecurity than in the past, particularly as benefits are linked to increasing conditional workfare. Conditionality opens the path for policymakers to depress access to benefits through the creation and manipulation of administrative burdens (Herd & Moynihan, 2019). The result is substantial shifts in the distributive structure of benefits within the working age populations, not just across generations.

Over time, these differences across age groups have also meant differences across different generations of citizens (Birnbaum et al., 2017). Today's older people, in some countries, have lived most of their lives with relatively generous benefits, whereas others have witnessed substantial growth or cutbacks over the life-cycle. Tomorrow's older people will have experienced more extensive protection through the life-cycle than past generations in some areas (e.g. parental leave, support for dual earner families) and less extensive protection in others (e.g. unemployment benefits), and will enter old age with stronger public pension systems than past cohorts in some countries (e.g. Canada) and weaker ones in others (e.g. Germany).

Despite these varying policy shifts, the broad cross-place and over-time patterns raise an important set of puzzles. Why have countries largely refrained from overt and visible cuts to benefits for older people, but at the same time failed to invest in *healthy ageing*? Put differently, why are the win-win policies that constitute a key route to healthy ageing relatively limited, even as policymakers have ostensibly looked to protect benefits for older people?

4.3 The Politics of Healthy Ageing

The previous section argued that healthy ageing requires thinking about the distribution of resources across the life-cycle and across places, not just focusing on old-age. Systems that seemingly concentrate 'too many' resources on older people, by failing to invest in the capacities and health of younger populations, or 'too few' resources on the older people by failing to stem social exclusion and poverty among older people, may not necessarily be mis-allocating resources across generations, but under-investing in healthy ageing altogether.

Addressing both income risks and the quality of public services over the life-cycle is expensive, and calls for a large and extensive policy apparatus. While the fiscal costs of pursuing win-win policies are an obvious and central part of any explanation as to why they are limited across time and place, costs alone are not enough to explain these patterns. As outlined above, in the period of welfare expansion some countries moved to expand benefits for younger and older groups in tandem, whereas others did not. Equally, in the more recent era some countries have trimmed working age benefits more extensively than those for the elderly, and others have not. Moreover, as argued elsewhere in this book, while ageing has created some generic costs pressures, the extent of demographic change does not in itself require a particular adjustment path (or rule out increasing taxes). Collectively, these shifts raise the question of what types of political configurations shape different adjustment paths.

The following sub-sections make two arguments. First, a large body of work in political science argues that the political coalitions that allow age-focused policies to emerge and persist often also *undercut* coalitions around healthy ageing. We make sense of this seeming disjuncture between the age-bias of policymaking and the bias against healthy ageing by arguing that to understand the politics of healthy ageing, we need to see ageing policy as a form of redistribution with class, regional and gender implications. Attention to age-based cleavages – often expressed via conflict between insiders and outsiders – can work to demobilize attention to class, regional and gender inequalities. It thus makes constructing a distributive 'win-win' coalition more difficult.

Second, and somewhat ironically, the places with the healthiest ageing potential are those that empower broader and more youth-inclusive political coalitions, which in turn have tended to build more inclusive welfare states, institutionalize longer-time horizons and provide a balance of policies that invest in the future and alleviate poverty and insecurity in the present. Where 'win-win coalitions' have emerged in more recent years, they have often done so through cross-class coalitions built around addressing gender (or other forms of) inequality, rather than exclusively addressing older voters.

4.3.1 Why is the Win-Win So Difficult to Achieve?

What explains the age focus of many welfare states? A first line of work, pioneered by Lynch (2006), looks to explicitly examine the age orientation of the welfare state as it emerged in the early era of welfare expansion, through the interwar and post-war period. Lynch asks why some countries developed welfare programmes largely via benefits targeted to older people, leading to a high degree of redistribution among older people but a lower corresponding level of spending on the working age population, while others expanded benefits more evenly across age groups.

To explain these choices, Lynch turns to the structure of early programmes and the nature of subsequent party competition. She argues that where early reformers introduced more citizenship-based welfare benefits and political parties subsequently competed for new voters on programmatic lines, parties had an incentive to expand programmes to younger people through citizenship-based policies. By contrast, in countries with more particularistic forms of party competition, parties had fewer incentives to expand programmes beyond existing programmatic insiders, maintaining an older age structure in benefits. The Netherlands is a key example of the former structure, and Italy of the latter dynamic, something that continues to show up in the contemporary data outlined by Figure 4.3.

For Lynch, the structure of party competition and welfare state grow together with a reinforcing logic, in some cases encouraging political parties to expand programmes to attract new voters, while in others to maintain them to retain existing voters. The result is substantial cross-time continuity in the age orientation of the welfare state, with early programme choices having a reinforcing effect. In this framing, 'win-win' policies are possible, but they are, in many ways, the historical exception. The growth of programmatic competition in already universalistic systems is a particularly Northern European phenomenon – with more patronage-oriented party systems, or less stable forms of competition, in much of the globe. Crucially, Lynch shows that in these former cases, more inclusive coalitions emerged behind political parties that allowed them to move beyond targeted appeals to existing constituents.

A second line of work turns from the historical development of the welfare state to its more recent developments, asking explicitly how politicians navigate distributional tradeoffs – including intergenerational tradeoffs – in an era of fiscal constraint.

One stream of work suggests that under these constraints, 'win-win' policies may be particularly difficult due to the time horizons of political actors. The payoff – both politically and economically – to investment in healthy ageing may not manifest for a generation, as younger citizens gain skills and older citizens enter old age in better health, but the costs of spending are borne in the present. While expanding programmes to the young in the present has immediate political rewards, many of the benefits with regard to long-term health and productivity require the longer-time horizons relative to immediate costs. This inter-temporal gap can be politically difficult to navigate, giving leaders little ability to claim credit in the present, but having to ask voters to pay upfront costs in terms of increased taxes or other forms of cuts in spending.

Alan Jacobs (2011) asks under what conditions policymakers can make choices that 'govern for the long-term'. While long-term expansion and investment are difficult, as Jacobs and others studying pensions show, the long-time horizon policymakers have engaged in both cuts and 'recalibration' to pensions and other systems, often with long-term effects, thus long-term is not impossible but difficult. Jacobs' approach does not necessarily predict age-skewed policy, but does suggest that some aspects of win-win policies can be politically difficult.

Jacobs argues that political systems can give actors incentives to invest in long-term solutions – but only under certain conditions. For Jacobs, longer term policies only emerge when policymakers are simultaneously electorally secure, have clear models about the impact of future policies and inhabit institutions that allow policy reforms. Where politicians are less electorally secure, future costs and benefits to policies more contested, or the institutions of political decision-making limit decisive actions, politicians are less willing and able to make inter-temporal tradeoffs. While Jacobs' argument points in a number of directions for explaining shifts, he too emphasizes that broad coalitions, including interest groups with longer time horizons, are key to explaining when politicians can navigate short-termism.

A third line of work further probes the political alignments around expanding different types of spending in the present. A number of recent studies have looked to theorize expenditure on age groups in terms of an electoral tradeoff between social investment and social consumption (Beramendi et al., 2015; Garritzmann et al., 2018) and the relative preferences for orthodox economic policy in an ageing population (Vlandas, 2017). This work argues that different groups of voters prioritize varying forms of expenditure, largely based on their interests in – or outside – the labour market.

Under this tradeoff framing, differences in prioritization emerge by skill, income and age groups for 'investment' versus 'consumption' policies. Older voters and older working age voters, especially those in relatively secure jobs, tend to prioritize existing forms of spending on pensions and unemployment insurance. This group has a strong material interest in income transfers that secure their wellbeing, and sees fewer immediate direct benefits to reforms that expand education and training for younger people. By contrast, educated younger people, and some categories of labour market 'outsiders' – those without permanent or secure employment contracts – prefer spending on investment policies like education and active labour market programmes that promise to expand their opportunities in the labour force.

This approach, then, starts from the premise that win-win configurations are often not possible due to constraints on spending, and frames the choice between types of spending as a distributive struggle across age groups and types of workers. While both insiders and outsiders in an unconstrained setting might prefer both forms of spending, where spending is constrained they prioritize differently. This work builds on an older literature suggesting that so-called labour market insiders (which includes former insiders who are now retired) in Europe are a powerful bulwark against welfare state change, including changes involving investment in more 'youth'-oriented policies (Rueda, 2015).

Where insiders and older voters hold more sway, the age orientation will remain skewed to older voters, but these same voters might prevent straight-out cuts and a reduction in the size of the welfare state. In general, this work suggests that insiders tend to have more structural power than outsiders. Both because of their links to traditional left parties and unions (Thelen, 2014), long-standing mobilization as 'policy takers' (Pierson, 1996) and higher propensity to vote (Goerres, 2007), the policy process is more likely to respond to the demands of these groups. The result then, is a relative under-investment in youth-based policies, and many of the pre-requisites to healthy ageing.

Collectively, this literature suggests that 'win-win' policies are very difficult for three reasons: (a) programmes are highly path dependent because the politics that produce them are further reproduced through them, with loss-averse voters and interest groups mobilizing to protect the status quo; (b) voters and politicians face short time horizons, which may be further shortened under conditions of electoral threat from actors explicitly supporting consumption over investment; and (c) sizeable parts of the voting public prioritize current consumption of passive social benefits, which benefits the current older population, but not necessarily healthy ageing. While all three of the above approaches suggest that age matters politically, each also suggests that understanding age requires embedding the politics of ageing in a broader political context that looks at how age intersects with existing welfare structures, the nature of partisan political competition and other forms of mobilized political inequalities. Where existing welfare structures benefit insiders, parties have stable support bases and intergenerational inequalities are pitted against other forms of social and economic inequality, more age-focused institutions are likely to emerge and stay in place.

Building on these claims, the following section shows that where age-based policies are politicized in broader equality-promoting coalitions, particularly those seeking gender equality, win-win policies are possible.

4.4 Coalitions and Healthy Ageing

The above section suggested win-win policies are difficult to achieve, but some countries have maintained or moved towards them over time, while others have not. What can we learn from those that have introduced such policies? The following section argues that (a) creating win-win outcomes requires broad social coalitions that combine intra- and intergenerational interests, and (b) this combination often involves incorporating actors that explicitly mobilize both sets of issues. Historically, gender-based advocacy groups have played a crucial role, because of their centrality in politicizing both family and labour market issues – drawing together redistributive and intergenerational claims. To see these dynamics, we turn to several instances of reforms towards more 'win-win' outcomes.

The Scandinavian countries have long stood out as key developers of 'social investment'-style policies, and at the forefront of healthy ageing. Lynch (2006) shows that these welfare states have long had a younger structure. However, the move towards social investment in the Scandinavian countries emerged extensively in the 1970s and 1980s, with expansion of benefits targeted at supporting women's entry into the labour force.

This early expansion of parental leave and childcare services – as well as more extensive home and institutional care for the elderly – built on a larger shift in the underlying political coalitions underpinning not just social policy and the welfare state. Sweden, for instance, had relatively under-developed early childhood programmes in the 1960s and 1970s, compared to other European countries (Morgan, 2002). However, the expansion of demand for female workers, combined with new demands from feminist groups, put childcare and parental leave policies on the agenda through the 1970s.

These demands were, however, not narrowly targeted at the state. Thelen (2014) describes the process of change in these countries (focusing in particular on Denmark) in terms of 'embedded flexibilization'. She argues that as women began to enter the labour force, unions representing the public sector and service workers developed more extensive relationships with the traditionally male-dominated manufacturing sector. As the size of the service sector grew, this relationship meant increasing institutional links in wage bargaining between lower productivity labour-intensive service jobs and blue-collar manufacturing jobs. In other words, unions representing public sector workers, an increasingly female workforce, institutionalized more pay equity in the labour market, creating substantial *intragenerational* redistribution.

As parties across the political spectrum turned to emphasizing support for female labour force participation and expanded childcare and parental leaves, this also meant more support for *intergenerational* equity – as the already developed system of pensions was complemented with benefits targeting young parents and children (Gingrich & Ansell, 2015). The result was a robust expansion of a range of social investment policies, without an initial erosion on benefits for the elderly. Put differently, while insider-outsider divides remain relevant in the Scandinavian labour market and in individual voting behaviour (e.g. Lindvall & Rueda, 2014), the early development of broader coalitions built around women in the public sector (and private service sector), in both the labour movement and electorally, allowed the emergence of more extensive life-cycle policy.

This scenario has changed somewhat over time. Successive governments in a number of Scandinavian countries have trimmed unemployment and pension benefits; and, for instance, in Sweden, the Conservative-led Reinfeldt government substantially cut taxes. Moreover, the marketization of care services, and the broader shift towards more limited institutional care, has meant some changes in the access of services for the elderly (Gingrich 2011). Nonetheless, there remains a strong focus in these welfare states on benefits and services that promote both inter-generational and intra-generational solidarity.

This emphasis shows itself in the nature of political competition. Figure 4.5 demonstrates the number of mentions of welfare and education

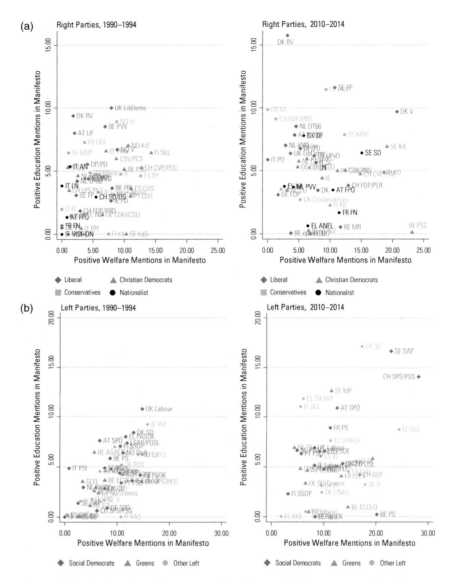

Figure 4.5 The number of mentions of welfare and education in political manifestos, by country.

Source: Volkens et al., 2020

in political manifestos, by country, as measured by the Comparative Manifestos Project (CMP). The CMP data do not allow us to disaggregate discussions of age groups explicitly, thus we use overall positive mentions of welfare and overall positive mentions of education as a proxy for attention to different age groups. What Figure 4.5 shows is that over time, parties on the Scandinavian left, and to a lesser extent the right as well, have become increasingly positive towards both education and welfare, with parties elsewhere pursuing mixed paths on both dimensions. Even in an era of cutbacks, the attention to wellbeing across the life-cycle in Sweden and Denmark, for instance, is high in comparative terms.

Thelen (2014) contrasts the Scandinavian case to that of continental Europe, particularly Germany, where insider-outsider cleavages continued to dominate through the 1990s and 2000s in both the labour market and electoral politics. Here, the traditional manufacturing unions initially took a less inclusive and coordinating approach to lower wage service workers, allowing increasing wage drift between the manufacturing sector and the low-skilled service sector. Politically, through this time period, as Beramendi and Rueda (2007) argue, the mainstream left also continued to largely represent traditional insiders.

However, even here, where shifts have occurred towards investment-type policies over the life-cycle, they have built on broader coalitions of younger groups who have often explicitly pushed for greater gender equity and support for family policy. The relatively substantial expansion of childcare in Germany through the 2000s followed in part through the growth of a more electorally mobile female and high skilled electorate (Fleckenstein, 2011; Morgan, 2013). These policies were led in part by the centre-right (the CDU in Germany) and were particularly favourable to higher-skilled women, but nonetheless demonstrate a dynamic of change in which demands for greater gender equity promote a reorientation towards more life-cycle policies. Abou-Chadi and Wagner (2020) find the move towards investment policies can yield electoral gains for the left as well, but only when paired with moderation on 'second dimension' issues like cultural liberalism and gender equity. Particularly in proportional electoral systems, where younger urban voters face less of an aggregation penalty (compared to majoritarian systems, where such voters are 'over concentrated' in cities), voters concerned about gender issues as well as other distributive issues are more able to select parties that put these questions on the agenda.

Häusermann (2010) shows how possible coalitions of insiders and outsiders, particularly built around gender, can also change the distributive space around benefits in the interest group sphere. Her work examines pension reforms in a number of continental European countries. Contra early work suggesting pensions are 'un-reformable', Häusermann finds that many continental European countries did engage in substantial pension reform, sometimes expanding equity through new pension credits and at other times limiting it. Groups representing women, or broader concerns about gender equity, also played a critical role in this process, albeit to different distributive ends – sometimes facilitating cuts in coalition with centre-right parties and other times expansion.

Why have gender issues been important to new coalitions around the welfare state? Women, like older people, are a heterogeneous group, both in terms of their economic and political behaviours. However, attention to women's historic exclusion from the welfare state, particularly where benefits ran through 'male breadwinners', and the labour market has brought the possibility of new political and interest group coalitions around expansionary life-cycle policies without an immediate erosion of benefits for the elderly.

The tradeoff framework, reviewed above, assumes either a strong budget constraint, no macro-economic effects of investment, and thus a hard tradeoff between expanding investment and maintaining consumption. However, within a family, investment and consumption can be two sides of the same coin (albeit a costly one). Programmes that look to support female participation in the labour force often must bridge the caring needs of both young children and older people. Where this support is done through extensive public policies (rather than more limited forms of tax breaks or credits for caring), it can produce both investment in the skills of the female labour force and consumption for the elderly. The gendered nature of caring (both in the home and the paid labour force) means that attention to wages in the care sector, support and funding for care and family policies can all have the dual effect of expanding benefits for the young while also providing resources to older recipients. Equally, in the area of pensions, in attending to women's more historically uneven participation in the paid labour force, Häusermann points to the uneven access to benefits among the elderly and recognition of career differences over the life-cycle.

In short, women's historic position in the family has meant that attention to gender equity draws on many intergenerational issues, bringing a more life-course perspective into political discourse. This perspective has sometimes led to win-win policies – with attention to both intergenerational and intragenerational equity – but not always. The Swedish and Danish cases, then, remind us of the key importance of broader coalitions. Where win-win policies have emerged, they have drawn on both the interests of female workers and family policy in conjunction with concerns about equity in the labour market. However, these broad coalitions do not always emerge. Indeed, as Figure 4.6 shows, many moderate left and right parties are much more positive, in relative terms, towards education than towards welfare programmes, and family and education policies are sometimes expanded alongside cuts in other types of spending.

This observation brings us to the last section of the paper, returning to questions of class and other forms of inequality at the heart of ageing policy.

4.5 New Challenges

The above section argued that attention to gender equity has, in many European countries, brought more attention to questions of intergenerational solidarity. However, this intergenerational focus is not always accompanied by more attention to intragenerational equity. This chapter concludes with a discussion of two increasingly important issues that highlight the intersection of class and region with intergenerational solidarity. These issues, like the more generic focus on life-course policies discussed above, will be crucial to future healthy ageing.

First, many European countries, including both the older and newer EU member states, have experienced increases in not just income inequality in recent years but also wealth inequality. A large part of this increase has been driven by a boom in asset prices, particularly house prices (Fuller et al., 2020). This growing wealth inequality has clear age-based implications. Older people are more likely to own substantial assets, and in many cases have benefited from appreciation in house prices, but have been harmed by low interest rates on other forms of saving, while younger people are 'locked out' of increasingly expensive housing markets.

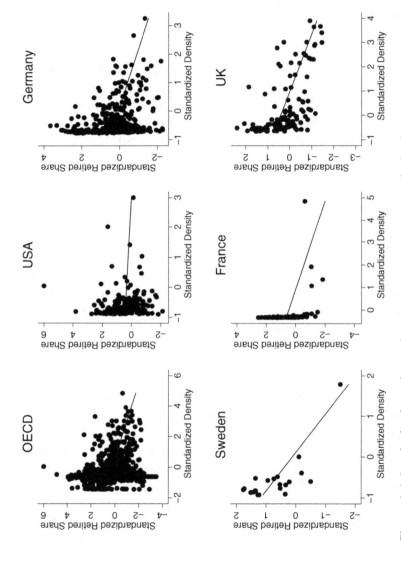

Figure 4.6 Standardized population density versus country-year standardized age structure, NUTS-3 levels or equivalent, 2016.

Despite the seeming potential for new generational divisions over housing, and wealth more generally, the politics of such shifts have often been 'refamilializing', forcing young people to rely on family wealth – where they can. Bohle and Seabrooke (2020) describe these shifts, in extremis, in terms of 'housing as patrimony'. This reliance highlights one of the key features of the political economy of healthy ageing: what appears as a generational conflict over resources often has a core source in other forms of inequality. Wealth divides that create ostensible intergenerational tension often rest on deeper class divisions. Those who started out wealthier – who had access to assets in the first place – have benefited the most. Bohle and Seabrooke argue that where policymakers in Europe both cut back many social benefits and pursued policies expanding wealth generation, the result has been both rising inequality and reliance on the family.

The politics of family wealth have long been a key issue in Southern Europe, particularly in countries like Italy that combine rigid housing markets and high levels of youth unemployment, reproducing both class- and age-based inequalities within and across generations. However, the rapid rise of house prices across the Scandinavian and Anglo countries may portend further shifts along these lines. For instance, Ansell (2014) finds that house price appreciation can push more conservative voters further to the right on social policy and spending, potentially reducing the scope for political coalitions around either form of solidarity. In other words, what appears initially as a potential source of intergenerational conflict rests on a broader set of questions about the future distribution of economic resources both across and within generations – a distribution that will affect the wellbeing of the elderly and of younger generations.

These issues have become particularly pronounced for a second reason: that of growing regional inequality in some cases. While overall regional inequality varies across Europe (both in its level and cross-time trends), house prices have appreciated in particular in Europe's capital regions and densest urban areas, in part due to the rise of the knowledge economy and new economic sectors clustered in urban areas. A growing body of work points to the changing spatial structure of economic growth (Krugman, 1991) and its political consequences (Beramendi, 2012; Iversen & Soskice, 2019). This rise of more post-industrial economic structures has promoted growth in urban areas, leading to some out-migration of working age adults from declining regions.

At present, urban-rural gaps in unmet need are not large, but may become larger in the future as declining areas increasingly become home to a larger share of older people. Figure 4.6 shows this connection. Using small regions (NUTS3 in Europe and equivalent regions elsewhere), it shows the country-year standardized population density versus country-year standardized age structure in 2016. We see that the large dense cities are much younger in many countries, meaning that less dense areas, which are generally experiencing lower levels of overall growth, are often the places where care needs and health needs will be more pronounced. Solidarity among and within generations, then, requires attention not just to income support for each group, but to the quality of services provided in particular areas.

Investing in rural and elderly-heavy areas, however, faces both economic and political limits. As population growth in these areas slows, they may experience a pronounced slowing of private investment (which is already weak by historical standards, relative to the cost of borrowing). This outcome suggests that without some public investment, these regions are likely to face particular long-run disadvantages, disadvantages that could have a strong age component. However, as parties on the left have historically thrived more in cities, and do so even more in the contemporary moment, and parties on the mainstream and more populist right are more sceptical of expanding taxes or public debt, the question of regional cross-age coalitions around public investment is uncertain politically.

Put differently, whereas attention to gender, in politicizing the family, brought intergenerational solidarity onto the agenda, housing and growing urban-rural variation also have inter- and intragenerational components, but the class and regional dynamics around them may split, rather than pull together, coalitions around life-cycle policies and healthy ageing. How future generations will navigate these questions remains to be seen.

4.6 Conclusion

When we look across time and place, older people as a whole have been key 'winners' from the expansion of the welfare state. In large part this is a simple cohort effect: those whose formative years were spent in thriving and relatively equal economies move through life with a better situation than those whose formative years were in the post-1980s era of increasing inequality, a difference exacerbated by the many countries that have chosen to spend money on avoiding poverty among older people. Behind this broad pattern lie substantial differences in terms of how equal these gains have been amongst the elderly and the degree to which they build on solidarity with other age groups. As such, even where the elderly are major recipients, the policies in place aren't always optimal for healthy ageing – as healthy ageing requires attention to inequality: inequality amongst the elderly and inequality in the population as a whole.

In order to understand why these patterns emerge, we need to examine how politics often does cement intergenerational conflict (through insider-outsider dynamics) and how this conflict, far from preserving the needs of the elderly, often undercuts healthy ageing. When we look at places where a broader life-course perspective emerged, it often drew on cross-generation (and sometimes cross-class) coalitions around gender. Recognizing the need for these coalitions, and paying attention to the changing class and regional issues at the core of healthy ageing, will be crucial going forward.

Unequal Ageing: the Politics of Ageing As the Politics of Health Inequalities

5.1 Introduction

One major implication of the previous two chapters is that the politics of ageing is actually the politics of inequality – not a chimera of intergenerational inequality, but rather the inequalities that scholars of politics, social policy and health have long studied and understood (Lynch, 2020). As chapter two showed, one of the problematic assumptions of the 'ageing crisis' narrative is precisely the belief that older populations are homogeneous in their experience and outlook. This ignores the significant health inequalities which exist amongst older populations and overlooks the degree to which the costs of an ageing population are actually rooted in these inequalities. Without this framing, debates about intergenerational inequalities and the 'ageing crisis' are a distraction from both the deep social inequalities that exist in terms of gender, geography, race and ethnicity, socioeconomic status and the ways in which these social inequalities produce inequities in health. Intentional or not, to focus on intergenerational inequalities diverts attention from the real inequalities that shape people's lives and the politics of ageing and health.

These inequality-generating processes are not only located at one point in the life-course, of course. Health inequalities among older populations are the cumulative product of particular trajectories through the social spaces which create social and economic advantage and disadvantage. Indeed, one of the most profound implications of this emphasis on the 'ageing crisis' is that it has a tendency to obfuscate the continuing inequalities in who gets to be 'old' and who gets to enjoy good health in retirement. In this respect, the politics of ageing is more properly framed as the politics of inequality – and this cuts across generations.

In this chapter we draw out this argument by illuminating both the shape and scope of health inequalities across the life course and describing the causes of health inequalities. This is not an exhaustive overview of this large literature but instead we aim to provide a picture of how ignoring inequalities in health among children and the working-age population lays the foundation for the ageing crisis that concerns politicians and think tanks. We begin by examining inequalities in who gets to be old across a number of socio-demographic characteristics before offering a theory of the causes of health inequalities.

5.2 Unequal Ageing: Who Gets to Be Old?

Ageing and becoming 'old' are not universal experiences. There are significant social inequalities across the population in terms of life expectancy and disability-free life expectancy by gender, geography, race and ethnicity, socioeconomic status, etc. Health inequalities exist along many of the axes which divide and organize social life. There are geographical inequalities in health (e.g. by country, region or neighbourhood), and sex- or gender-based inequalities too. Inequalities in health cut across income, class, occupation and education, and they affect different racial groups. Health inequalities are systematic, avoidable and unfair differences in health (Whitehead, 1991).

5.2.1 Gender Inequalities in Health

In many countries women live longer than men – for example, life expectancy for women in Albania is over 4 years higher than for men (Albanian men 77.5 years, women 81.9 years); similarly, on average German women live ~5 years longer than American men (83.2 years compared to 78.4 years). Figure 1.2 in the introductory chapter shows how serious these inequalities can be, with the case of Lithuania representative of the many countries with dramatic gender inequalities in life expectancy.

Longer female life expectancies do not, however, mean better health. Women (particularly older women) also generally experience worse health: women get sick, men die (Doyal, 1995). For example, in France more men than women consider their health to be 'good' (70.2 per cent for men and 65.6 per cent for women). Limiting long-term conditions tend to be higher amongst older women than amongst older men. Women also have higher rates of mental ill-health, particularly in terms of depression and anxiety across all age groups. However, suicide rates are higher amongst men (Daykin & Jones, 2008). Health differences between men and women are partly explained in biological terms (i.e. sex-based) and partly in social terms (i.e. gender-based). Sex refers to the biological differences between men and women, whilst gender is the social construction of sex-related roles and relationships – how men and women are expected to act within particular societies (Hill, 2016).

Research on differences in health between men and women focuses on the interaction of these two different elements, although the social tends to be privileged. For example, men's poorer longevity is ascribed by some to men's higher rates of risky health behaviours such as alcohol consumption and drug abuse, or to the fact that men are less likely than women to access health care services (Annandale & Hunt, 2000). These are linked to gendered assumptions of what it means to be a 'man' within dominant forms of masculinity. Social factors are also important as women have less access to higher paid jobs and therefore less access to health-promoting resources. Employment is often gendered, with men and women therefore experiencing different working conditions. Women also continue to bear the brunt of the unpaid domestic labour and caring responsibilities. Institutional or structural sexism is also important (Homan, 2019). For example, studies have shown that in countries where men and women are more equal, the health of both men and women tends to be better (Reeves et al., 2016; Van de Velde et al., 2013).

5.2.2 Ethnic Inequalities in Health

Health also varies by race and ethnicity (Nazroo & Williams, 2006). For example, in the Netherlands all-cause mortality rates are more than ~1.2 times higher for Turkish, Surinamese and Antillean/Aruban males even after adjusting for other factors (Bos et al., 2004). In the USA African-Americans have a life expectancy four years lower than that of White Americans (Arias, 2011), whilst indigenous populations in the USA, Canada, New Zealand and Australia experience life expectancies of seven to twelve years less than their non-indigenous counterparts (Hill, 2016).

Non-white populations tend to suffer a greater burden of morbidity as well. American Whites spend a greater share of their years free of activity limitations (Molla, 2013). Importantly, morbidity and mortality disparities between Whites and African-Americans shrink and gradually disappear over the life-course. Among the very old, African-Americans appear to enjoy a health advantage over Whites. This phenomenon, referred to as the racial morbidity and mortality crossover, is the subject of an ongoing scientific debate. While some scholars have hypothesized that the crossover may be a measurement artefact, others have argued that adverse life-course selection translates to better overall health of the oldest African-Americans.

Sociologists and social epidemiologists have persuasively demonstrated that a large share of today's observed racial and ethnic differences in health are due not to innate biological differences between members of different racial and ethnic groups but to social and environmental factors. For example, Cooper and colleagues (2005) showed that while US Whites have lower prevalence of hypertension than African-Americans, they have greater prevalence of hypertension than Blacks living in Africa. In contrast, African-Americans have higher hypertension rates than populations of predominantly White European countries, such as Sweden and Italy, but lower than others, including Germany and Finland. Because wealth and socioeconomic resources tend to be unevenly distributed in racially and ethnically stratified societies socioeconomic status interacts with racial and ethnic disparities. In the US context, the median net worth of a White household is nearly nine times greater than that of a Black household and five times greater than that of a Hispanic household. Asian-American households' median net worth exceeds that of Whites by 1.4 times (Eggleston & Munk, 2019). The large disparities between people of different races, partly reflect economies and social policies in which socioeconomic resources are distributed by race.

Prior research has shown that even after adjusting for socioeconomic status, morbidity and mortality disparities by race/ethnicity remain. Perhaps surprisingly, racial health disparities are larger among the more privileged than the less privileged, whose outcomes are more uniform (Braveman et al., 2010). Racism and racial discrimination likely account for a share of the health outcome differences between similarly advantaged White and non-White populations (D. R. Williams et al., 2019). As an upstream cause of disadvantage, racism and racial discrimination may influence health through multiple pathways. For example, racial segregation can limit access to healthful neighbourhoods and desirable housing options, and has usually been linked to worse health in Blacks, including worse pregnancy outcomes and increased mortality (Kramer & Hogue, 2009). Discrimination has been shown to reduce access to goods, services and health care in multiple national contexts

(Ben et al., 2017). In addition, experiences of discrimination may also have a less immediately apparent effect – they are likely to increase individual stress and translate to higher allostatic load (Allen et al., 2019), which has been connected to the emergence of multiple chronic conditions (McEwen & Stellar, 1993).

5.2.3 Socioeconomic Inequalities in Health

Socioeconomic status is a term that refers to occupational class, income or educational level (Bambra, 2011). Across Europe, people with higher occupational status (e.g. professionals such as teachers or lawyers) have better health outcomes than those with lower occupational status (e.g. manual workers). Similarly, people with a higher income or tertiary-level education have better health outcomes than those with a low income or no educational qualifications (Bambra, 2016). Current levels of health inequalities in Europe are depicted in Figures 5.1, 5.2 and 5.3.

Figure 5.1 shows inequalities in general health by income group. Good health increases with income in all countries (Forster et al., 2018). At the EU level, 60.0 per cent of people with a low income report to be in good health compared to 78.3 per cent of people with a high income: a difference of over 18 percentage points. Figure 5.1 also shows how inequalities in general health vary across Europe. For example, the health gap is 20 percentage points in Ireland and Portugal but almost 40 in Lithuania.

Figure 5.2 shows educational inequalities in long-term chronic diseases (non-communicable diseases) (McNamara et al., 2017). Again, there are clear inequalities across Europe. For instance, someone with a low education is over three times more likely than someone with a tertiary education to report depression. As Figure 5.2 also indicates, educational inequalities in Europe are highest for depression, diabetes and obesity.

There are also socioeconomic inequalities in health-related practices: rates of smoking and alcohol consumption are higher in lower socioeconomic groups, whilst rates of physical activity and consumption of fruit and vegetables are lower (Huijts et al., 2017). For example, as Figure 5.3 shows, smoking follows a clear social gradient: in all European countries except Portugal the likelihood of smoking daily is higher for individuals with a primary or secondary education than for their more highly educated peers (Huijts et al., 2017).

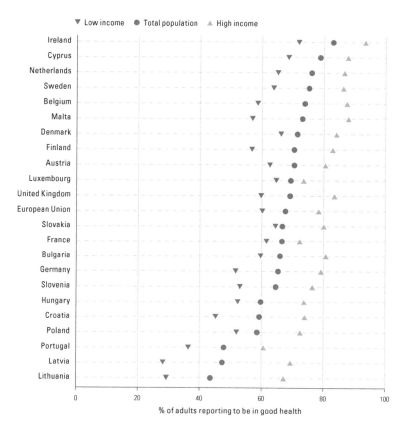

Figure 5.1 Income inequalities in self-reported health across Europe, 2016.

Notes: Data refer to 2016.

Source: Forster et al., 2018, reproduced with permission of authors

5.2.4 Geographical Inequalities in Health

It is well known that health varies between countries. Most notably, there are considerable differences between the richest and the poorest European countries. For example, average life expectancy for men and women in countries like France is high (over 83 years), while in Latvia or Lithuania it is significantly lower (~75 years in both). The USA, the richest country in the world, has more than four years less life expectancy than Japan and an infant mortality rate that is three times greater than that of Iceland (Schrecker & Bambra, 2015). This has led to discussions of a 'US health disadvantage' whereby the USA has worse

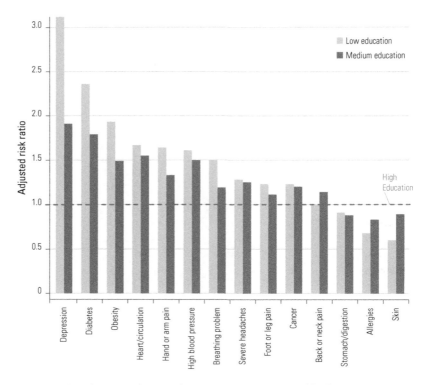

Figure 5.2 Educational inequalities in non-communicable diseases in Europe.

Notes: Age-adjusted risk ratios estimate the probability of self-reporting a particular NCD for individuals with low and medium education vis-à-vis highly educated people.

Source: Forster et al., 2018, reproduced with permission of authors

outcomes across a number of key health outcomes (such as obesity or heart disease) than other comparable wealthy countries (US National Research Council & US Institute of Medicine, 2013).

Within countries, there are also regional inequalities in health. For example, in Belgium in 2016 the standardized death rate per 100,000 was 886 deaths in the province of West Vlaanderen but in Hainaut it was 1,161 deaths (Forster et al., 2018). These regional inequalities in health are evident in all other countries. By way of example, Figure 5.4 shows regional inequalities in life expectancy across Europe for men and women combined. It shows that across Europe, all countries experience

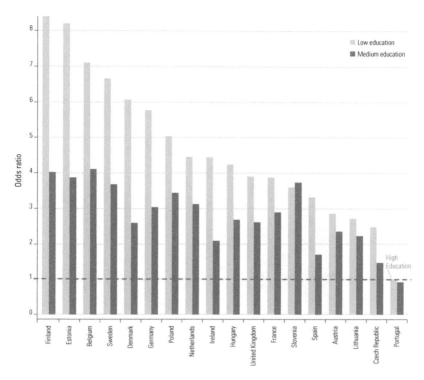

Figure 5.3 Probability of smoking by educational status.

Notes: Age- and sex-adjusted odds ratios represent the probability of being a daily smoker given low or medium education, respectively, relative to individuals with high education.

Source: Forster et al., 2018, reproduced with permission of authors

unequal health across their constituent regions. These patterns also exist outside Europe as, for example, in China, where average life expectancy is over five years less in the northern provinces than in the southern ones.

The most striking geographical inequalities in health, though, are those that exist between neighbourhoods, with neighbourhoods that are the most deprived (measured in terms of income, employment, health, education, crime, access to services and living environment) having worse health than those that are less deprived – and this follows a spatial gradient with each increase in deprivation resulting in a decrease in average health. In England the gap between the most and least deprived areas is around nine years average life expectancy and nineteen years average

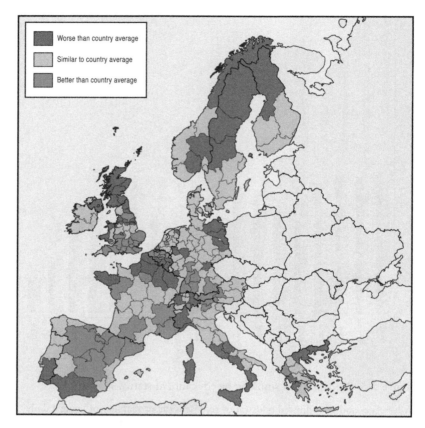

Figure 5.4 Average life expectancy by European region for men and women.

Source: reproduced from Bambra, 2016, with permission of Policy Press

healthy life expectancy for men and around seven and nineteen years respectively for women (ONS, 2018). In some cases these deprived and affluent areas with such differences in health outcomes can be located very closely together – indeed just a few miles apart, as with London, where life expectancies along a single Underground line, the Bakerloo Line, vary dramatically (Bambra, 2016).

5.2.5 Intersectional Inequalities

Health inequalities are also intersectional. Intersectionality is a way of looking at multiple influences on health (Gkiouleka et al., 2018). It focuses on how socioeconomic status, ethnicity and gender are experienced not separately but in combination and that we all have different aspects of social identity that coexist with one another. Focusing on any one element of inequality, such as patriarchy or White supremacy, risks obscuring the ways in which different inequalities interact.

Intersectionality therefore looks at the 'axes of inequality', particularly socioeconomic status, gender and ethnicity together. It also considers gender and ethnicity as social factors rather than simply demographic ones, viewing them as socially structured, constructed and experienced. So, for example, health differences between men and women arise not just because of biological differences but as a result of the social construction of sex-related roles and relationships (gender). Likewise, ethnic inequalities in health can arise through racism, with ethnic minority groups more likely to experience discrimination personally, institutionally (systematic exclusion and disadvantage) and economically. Health is therefore affected by each of these axes of inequality (Hill, 2016). Intersectionality therefore draws recognition to the fact that any individual has 'such multiple aspects of identity with relevance for their relationships with others and with the structures and systems of power – and, therefore, for their health'. Intersectionality looks at all aspects of the individual and how they experience the various aspects of their social identity within particular contexts, and with specific health effects. Black men, for example, have far poorer health than White women. These inequalities also intersect with age. While older people have poorer health than younger people, not all older people experience poor health in the same way. For example, ethnic minorities in France aged 65 and over were almost twice as likely (~40%) to report a heart or circulation problem than those who were members of the ethnic majority (~21%).

5.2.6 Trends in Health Inequalities

These intersecting inequalities have become crucial to political debates across high-income countries because they are behind the stagnation of life expectancy in some contexts. For example, stagnating life expectancy in the UK has been driven by a mix of rising mortality among both the elderly and, more surprisingly, those of working age. Perhaps more striking, inequalities in life expectancy have tragically risen in the last few years, according to recently released figures from the Office for National Statistics (ONS, 2019). There are also signs that inequalities in

nt mortality rates may also be increasing. This is not only because
reater improvements among the better-off but because the poorest
have seen real declines. In the most deprived parts of England, female
life expectancy at birth fell by almost 100 days between 2012–2014 and
2015–2017. Men in the poorest areas saw no improvements, while those
in the richest parts of the UK continued to see their life expectancies
improve. This is true among the elderly too.

In the USA all-cause mortality rates stopped falling around the turn
of the twenty-first century (Case & Deaton, 2015). The halt of mortality
improvements has been traced to increased mortality in middle-aged
non-Hispanic Whites. While mortality of Whites in the youngest and
oldest ages has continued to decline, as have mortality rates for Blacks
and Hispanics, their gains were overshadowed by rapid growth in what
Case and Deaton refer to as deaths of despair in middle-aged Whites:
drug overdoses, suicides and alcohol-related liver mortality. The mortality rate increase was accompanied by worsened self-rated health
and greater reports of chronic pain (Case & Deaton, 2015). The social
causes underlying the mortality rate increase in middle-aged Whites are
the subject of ongoing discussion. Case and Deaton argue that they are
symptoms of a cumulative disadvantage of working class Whites, including weakening labour market and social structures, as well as falling
marriage rates and lower participation in organized religion (Case &
Deaton, 2017). Others have leaned towards more macroeconomically
oriented explanations (Hollingsworth et al., 2017) or argued that the
main culprit behind increased drug-related mortality is increased availability of drugs (Ruhm, 2018). We explore this further in Chapter 6.

These trends in terms of stalling and indeed falling life expectancy in
the UK and Europe are also reflected in terms of trends in health inequalities. Since the global financial crisis of 2007–8, Europe has experienced
considerable economic, social and political upheaval. Across Europe
the economic recovery has been weak and inequitable: unemployment
has remained high, particularly amongst young adults and those with
low skills, wages have stagnated and living standards have declined.
Relatedly, health inequalities have also increased. Whilst average life
expectancy at birth in the European Union increased from 79.4 in 2008
to 81.0 in 2016, these increases were smaller amongst men and women
with a lower level of education (Forster et al., 2018). For example, in
Denmark the difference in life expectancy at age 30 between men with
a low education and men with a tertiary education rose from 4.8 years

to 6.4 years. The respective gap for women increased from 3.7 years to 4.7 years. So, whilst the health of everyone in Europe has improved over the last decade, more privileged groups have benefited the most, leading to increased health inequalities in some countries (Mackenbach et al., 2016).

5.2.7 COVID-19 Pandemic and Health Inequalities

These social inequalities in health by gender, geography, race and ethnicity, and socioeconomic status are evident across all health conditions, from mental health through to chronic diseases such as diabetes and heart disease, and even in infectious diseases including Covid-19 (Bambra et al., 2020; Bambra et al., 2021). There is clear evidence of social inequalities in COVID-19 infection and mortality rates from Spain, the USA and the UK. For example, intermediate data published by the Catalonian government in Spain in April 2020 suggests that the rate of COVID-19 infection is six or seven times higher in the most deprived areas of the region compared to the least deprived (Catalan Agency for Health Quality and Assessment, 2020). Similarly, in preliminary USA analysis, Chen and Krieger (2020) found area-level socio-spatial gradients in confirmed cases in Illinois and New York City, with dramatically increased mortality risk observed among residents of the most disadvantaged counties. Official national data in England and Wales found that coronavirus (COVID-19)-related deaths were twice as high in the most deprived neighbourhoods (55 per 100,000 population) than in the most affluent neighbourhoods (25 per 100,000 population) (ONS, 2020).

In regards to ethnic inequalities in COVID-19, data from England and Wales found that people who are Black, Asian and minority ethnic (BAME) accounted for around 35 per cent of 5,000 critically ill COVID-19 patients (in the period ending 16/4/2020) – although they only make up 14 per cent of the UK population (ICNARC, 2020). Similarly, there are large racial inequalities in COVID-19 infections and deaths in various US states and municipalities. For example, in Chicago (in the period ending 17/04/20), 60 per cent of COVID-19 deaths were amongst Black residents and the COVID-19 mortality rate for Black Chicagoans was 35 per 100,000 population compared to 8 per 100,000 population amongst White residents (City of Chicago, 2020). Gender also appears to be a risk factor for COVID-19 symptom severity and mortality, with data from many countries showing that mortality rates are much higher amongst men. For example, in March and April 2020 in England and Wales men made up 70 per cent of hospitalized cases and around 60 per cent of confirmed COVID-19-related deaths (ICNARC, 2020).

As the pandemic progresses, there will likely be an interaction of race, gender and socioeconomic inequalities, given the intersectionality of multiple aspects of social disadvantage (Gkiouleka et al., 2018).

5.3 What Causes Health Inequalities?

The explanations for different forms of health inequalities are rooted in the connection between health-related practices, material resources and institutions. These intersect with other features of the social world, such as socioeconomic status, place, gender and ethnicity. In the sections below, we focus on social position and place rather than gender and ethnicity. This is not because gender inequalities and ethnic inequalities are unimportant, but we focus on those which are most deeply connected to the ageing process generally and to our policy analysis in Chapter 6.

5.3.1 Material Resources: the Social Determinants of Health

'Materialist' explanations focus on the conditions which influence our access to health-enhancing goods, which limit our exposure to risk factors. Economic resources, for example, are one of these conditions because they can determine our ability to afford good quality services (e.g. hospitals, schools, transport infrastructure and social care) but also allow people to avoid materially harmful circumstances (e.g. poor housing, inadequate diet, physical hazards at work, environmental exposures). Fundamental cause theory (Phelan et al., 2010) is premised on the idea that money is fungible and therefore can be used to preserve inequalities, so if we address one specific inequality (e.g. lack of access to green spaces) overall health might improve as a result but income inequalities will lead to some other measurable health inequality increasing. Furthermore, runs the theory, new technology will often increase inequality: the benefits of wearable devices, for example, will accrue to better-off people first, which means that regardless of the intentions of the creators or the effect of the technology among users, most new health technologies will increase health inequalities.

The conditions which structure the social worlds in which we live, work, mature and die are commonly termed the 'social determinants of health'. Beside income, they include working conditions, housing and neighbourhood, labour market activity and access to certain goods and services, such as health care. Our social position in the world is a complex agglomeration of all of these aspects of our lives and so in a very meaningful sense people in different social positions inhabit quite distinct social and epidemiological life worlds.

One way in which our social position in the world influences health is through shaping our practices – how we live our lives. Health inequalities are grounded in everyday practices, both chosen and habitual. These practices are often called health behaviours (a term which can imbue social action with a degree of intentionality). However, social action is not always intentional and so we call them practices because these 'behaviours' often bear the hallmarks of a particular mode of engaging with the world which relies on pre-verbal understanding of what is appropriate in a given setting. Health-related practices, then, are ways people spend their time and also forms of consumption that affect health, including diet, exercise and other forms of consumption such as tobacco use. Practices are, of course, not solely determined by individual preferences. In fact, when we articulate our preferences we are usually expressing post-hoc justifications for habits that have not necessarily been subject to rational evaluation (Jerolmack & Khan, 2014). What we consume and how we spend our time is shaped by our social position because the 'worlds' we inhabit – whether we have a high income or not – make possible some forms of social action whilst making other practices more difficult. By cultivating distinct sets of practices, these 'worlds' can, as described above, have implications for health and health inequalities. When Mexicans leave cans of Coca-Cola on the graves of their ancestors on 'The Day of the Dead', they are revealing the value their community (or their social position in the world) places on specific forms of consumption.

The social nature of practices influences the size and shape of health inequalities and partially explains why the degree to which practices (or behaviours) influence health inequalities varies within and between countries over time. This is because practices are not inherently linked with inequalities per se. That is, specific practices only generate health inequalities if there are inequalities in who performs those practices. To come back to tobacco, smoking is a social practice which reflects gender roles, social class structures and income inequalities (Marron, 2017). So, as inequalities in smoking have decreased in Europe in recent decades, smoking has become a less important determinant of health inequalities. Crucially, there are important gender differences here because this decline has primarily been observed in men. This is not true of women, however, because inequalities in smoking among women have in fact increased (Gregoraci et al., 2017).

Practices differ between and within age groups. In 2014 the prevalence of 'current smokers' across the twenty-eight European member states was 32.6 per cent among 25–34 year olds and 26.7 per cent of 45–64 year olds. This ~6 percentage point gap is actually smaller than the 7 percentage point difference between the poorest income quintile and the richest quintile. In fact, the really striking difference is between income quintiles within specific age groups. There is a 13 percentage point gap in the prevalence of 'current smokers' between the poorest and the richest income quintiles among 25–34 year olds, and an 11.1 percentage point gap between the poorest and the richest income quintiles among those aged 55–64. These are differences that are going to have a profound influence on the costs of ageing in the future, and they are differences driven by the social determinants of health.

Finally, the social determinants of health may influence health outcomes through psychosocial pathways (Marmot, 2004). Beyond the materialist and practice-based explanations, the psychosocial is concerned with the psychic experience of social inequalities or other forms of social exclusion (Greer, 2018; Pickett & Wilkinson, 2010, 2015). The experience of discrimination or racism, for example, has profound negative effects on the health of the dominated racial group (D. R. Williams et al., 2019). Discrimination in the labour market leaves dominated racial groups in economically precarious positions, locked out of the mechanisms that ensure wealth accumulation (Shapiro, 2017). Self-reported discrimination is also associated with poorer mental health and (albeit less clearly) physical health as well (D. R. Williams et al., 2019).

A study using data from Norway compared the relative contribution of practices, material resources and psychosocial explanations (alongside biomedical factors) of socioeconomic (educational and income) inequalities in mortality. It concluded that material factors were the most important in explaining income inequalities in mortality whilst psychosocial and behavioural factors were the most important in explaining educational inequalities (Skalická et al., 2009). People exposed to one sort of factor (e.g. material) may also be exposed to another (e.g. psychosocial) and have interacting influences on their health. So, these explanations of health inequalities are intersecting rather than competing. Indeed, people of higher socioeconomic status (be it higher education levels, higher income or higher occupational class) have access to better resources, money, knowledge, prestige, power and beneficial social networks, whilst those of lower socioeconomic status (lower income, education or occupational class) have less access to such things. People of higher socioeconomic status also have access to better contexts (as shall be described in the next section) in terms of workplaces and neighbourhoods (Phelan et al., 2004). The health advantage of having a higher socioeconomic status is robust to varying degrees over time and place such that, whilst the clinical and proximal causes of socioeconomic inequalities in health have changed, the gradient still exists. For example, in the nineteenth century the leading causes of death were fevers and consumption, whilst in the twentieth and early twenty-first centuries the main causes of death are cancers and cardiovascular disease. Socioeconomic inequalities existed in the nineteenth century as they do today – despite the diversity of the actual causes of death. This is because high socioeconomic status in the nineteenth century enabled people to have better sanitation or to live away from polluting factories, for example, whilst in the twentieth and twenty-first centuries it enables better health-related practices or access to healthier work environments. People of high socioeconomic status use their resources to adapt to the disease threat of the day and gain a health advantage over those of lower socioeconomic status who do not have the resources to adapt. This has led to socioeconomic status being called a 'fundamental cause' of ill health – and ageing – which persists despite competing causes of death (Link & Phelan, 1995).

5.3.2 Explaining Geographic Inequalities in Health

Building on explanations of socioeconomic inequalities in health, researchers have traditionally explained geographical inequalities in health in terms of the effects of compositional (*who lives here?*) and contextual (*what is this place like?*) factors (Bambra, 2016). The compositional explanation asserts that the health of a given area, such as a town, region or country, is a result of the characteristics of the people who live there (individual-level demographic, health-related practices and socioeconomic factors). If more people smoke in a given area, then we would expect that area to have poorer health.

The contextual explanation, by contrast, argues that area-level health is also in part determined by the nature of the place itself in terms of its economic, social and physical environment. Health differs by place because it is also determined by the economic, social and physical environment of a *place*: *poor places lead to poor health*. Place mediates the way in which individuals experience social, economic and physical processes on their health: places can be salutogenic (health promoting) or pathogenic (health damaging) environments – place acts as a health ecosystem. These place-based effects can also be seen as the *collective* effects of the social determinants of health. That is, the socioeconomic position of the people who live in your community will impact your health irrespective of your own socioeconomic position. To capture these contextual effects, researchers commonly look at area poverty rates, unemployment rates, wages and types of work and employment in the area. The mechanisms whereby the economic profile of a local area impacts on health are multiple. For example, it affects the nature of work that an individual can access in that place (regardless of their own socioeconomic position). It also impacts on the services available in a local area, as more affluent areas will attract different services (such as food available locally or physical activity opportunities) than more deprived areas as businesses adapt to the different consumer demands in each area (see access to services in the opportunity structures section below). Area-level economic factors such as poverty are a key predictor of health, including cardiovascular disease, all-cause mortality, limiting long-term illness and health-related behaviours (Macintyre, 2007).

Places also have social aspects which impact on health. For example, local environments can shape our access to healthy – and unhealthy – goods and services, thus enhancing or reducing our opportunities to engage in healthy or unhealthy behaviours such as smoking, alcohol consumption, fruit and vegetable consumption or physical activity. Alongside access to services, another social aspect of place is collective social functioning. Collective social practices that are beneficial to health include high levels of social cohesion and social capital within the community. Social capital – '*the features of social organisation such as trust, norms, and networks that can improve the efficiency of society by facilitating coordinated actions*' (Putnam, 1993, 167) – has been put forward as a social mechanism through which place mediates the relationship between individual socioeconomic status and health outcomes (Hawe & Shiell, 2000). Some studies have found that areas with higher levels of social capital have better health, such as lower mortality rates, self-rated health, mental health and health behaviours. More negative collective effects can also come from the reputation of an area (e.g., stigmatized places can result in feelings of alienation and worthlessness) or the history of an area (e.g., if there has been a history of racial oppression). Residents of stigmatized places can also be discredited by association with these place characteristics. A notable and documented case of such place-based stigma is Love Canal, New York – the location of a toxic waste dump. Research has shown that such place-based stigma can result in psychosocial stress and associated ill health, alongside feelings of shame, on top of the physical health effects of air pollution such as respiratory disease (Airey, 2003).

Finally, place can also affect health through the nature of the physical environment (Marmot et al., 2008). There is a sizeable literature on the positive health effects of access to green space, as well as the negative health effects of waste facilities, brownfield or contaminated land, as well as air pollution (Bambra, 2016). One (in)famous example of the latter is the so-called *Cancer Alley* – the 87-mile stretch in the American state of Mississippi between Baton Rouge and New Orleans, the home of the largest petrochemicals site in the country (Markowitz & Rosner, 2003). In 2016 it was estimated that air pollution levels in London accounted for up to 10,000 unnecessary deaths per year (Walton et al., 2015). Another example of how the physical environment of areas varies is in respect to land pollution. A study found that in the American city of Baltimore mortality rates from cancer, lung cancer and respiratory diseases were significantly higher in neighbourhoods with larger amounts of brownfield land (Litt et al., 2002). The literature has also established the role of natural or green spaces as therapeutic or health-promoting landscapes. So, for example, studies have found that walking in natural, rather than urban, settings reduces stress levels and people residing in green areas report less poor health than those with less green surroundings (Maas et al., 2006). The unequal socio-spatial distribution of the environmental deprivation has also led to commentators developing the concept of environmental justice (Pearce et al., 2010). The fact that more deprived neighbourhoods are more likely to have air and land pollution and less likely to have green space can be seen as an aspect of social injustice (Pearce et al., 2010).

More recently, it has been acknowledged that the compositional and the contextual approaches are not mutually exclusive and that the health of places results from the interaction of people with the wider environment (*relational* approach) (Cummins et al., 2007). Indeed, separating them is an oversimplification and ignores the interactions between these two levels (Macintyre et al., 2002). The characteristics of individuals are influenced by the characteristics of the area. For example, occupational class can be determined by local school quality and the availability of jobs in the local labour market, or children might not play outside due to not having a private garden (a *compositional* resource), because there are no public parks or transport to get to them (a *contextual* resource) or because it might not be seen as appropriate for them to do so (*contextual* social functioning) (Macintyre et al., 2002). Similarly, areas with more successful economies (e.g. more high-paid jobs) will have lower proportions of lower socioeconomic status residents.

Further, the collective resources model suggests that all residents, and particularly those on a low income, enjoy better health when they live in areas characterized by more/better social and economic collective resources. This may be especially important for those on a low income as they are usually more reliant on local services. Conversely, the health of poorer people may suffer more in deprived areas where collective resources and social structures are limited, a concept known as deprivation amplification: the health effects of individual deprivation, such as lower socioeconomic status, can therefore be *amplified* by area deprivation (Macintyre, 2007).

These insights have profound implications for thinking about healthy ageing because the scarring effect of being born into a deprived community can linger long after people have moved away. Indeed, for the many people who stay in those communities, they are exposed to a series of disadvantages that impinge on their ability to live healthy lives. As Cummins and colleagues argue, '*there is a mutually reinforcing and reciprocal relationship between people and place*' which will structure how the costs associated with ageing are distributed geographically (Cummins et al., 2007, 1826). As we have already argued, ageing is not costly for everyone, but it is particularly costly for those communities where people spend more years in poor health. These negative health effects are experienced by everyone in those communities, but they are most keenly felt by those with the greatest individual disadvantage. It is already becoming clear that the costs of social care are not evenly distributed geographically, and such inequalities may widen if the upwardly mobile continue to move to major urban centres to access well-paid, more prestigious jobs.

5.4 Beyond the Social Position and Place: the Political Economy Approach

Socioeconomic and spatial inequalities are not random chance, however, because they are rooted in political and economic institutions (Besley & Kudamatsu, 2006; Greer et al., 2018; Lundberg, 2008). In 2014 the Lancet-University of Oslo Commission on Global Governance for Health put forward the concept of the 'political determinants of health', insisting that 'construing socially and politically created health inequities as problems of technocratic or medical management depoliticises social and political ills' (Ottersen et al., 2014, 636). The political economy approach argues that the social determinants of health (e.g., socioeconomic position and place) are themselves shaped by macro level structural determinants: politics, the economy, the (welfare) state, the organisation of work and the structure of the labour market (Bambra, 2011; Barnish et al., 2018) and that population health is shaped by the 'social, political and economic structures and relations' that may be, and often are, outside the control of the individuals they affect (Bambra et al., 2005; Krieger, 2001). Politics is understood here in its broadest terms as 'the process through which the production, distribution and use of scarce resources is determined in all areas of social existence' (Bambra et al., 2005), not simply as the actions of governments or political parties. Public health and health inequalities are thus considered to be politically determined with patterns of disease 'produced, literally and metaphorically, by the structures, values and priorities of political and economic systems ... Health inequities are thus posited to arise from whatever is each society's form of social inequality, defined in relation to power, property and privilege' (Krieger et al., 2013). In other words, why some places and people are consistently privileged whilst others are consistently marginalized is a political choice – it is about where the power lies and in whose interests that power is exercised. Political choices can thereby be seen as the *causes of the causes of the causes* of inequalities in health, both socioeconomic and spatial (Bambra, 2016).

To be more concrete, we can think of economic institutions as being concerned with the rules that govern who has access to the wealth produced by society, how the means of producing that wealth are organized, and the rules that govern competition in local and global markets. Taxes and transfers that pay for pensions, for example, can affect access to health care, and recent reductions in pension generosity in Europe are associated with rising inequalities in unmet medical need because the poorest experience reduced ability to afford health care whilst the richest experience no change (Reeves et al., 2017b). Minimum wage regulations constrain wage negotiations at the bottom of the income distribution and a number of papers have recently observed that the introduction of minimum wages improves mental health (Horn et al., 2017; Lenhart, 2017; Reeves, 2017b). Employment regulations that decommodify the labour market relations are associated with better health outcomes and lower absolute inequalities in health than countries which rely on more commodified market relationships (Beckfield & Krieger, 2009). Trade policy (Jarman, 2019; Jarman & Greer, 2010), which structures the rules that govern competition, may also influence health inequalities because they affect the social determinants of health (Barlow et al., 2017a; Blouin et al., 2009; Madureira Lima & Galea, 2018). For example, trade agreements alter food environments (Barlow et al., 2017b; Owen & Wu, 2007; Schram et al., 2015), expose some groups to long-term economic shocks (Rodrik, 2012) and may even harm infant mortality (Barlow, 2018).

Political institutions are also commonly 'listed alongside ... other fundamental causes' of health, albeit often without elaborating on 'what these political forces might be [or] how they operate' (Torres & Waldinger, 2015). The theoretical reasoning connecting political institutions and health is relatively 'straightforward' (Bollyky et al., 2019). Political institutions influence population health because countries with free and fair elections, for example, make politicians more responsive to the preferences of citizens and this could influence policy decisions and the structure of economies, both of which may impact health and wellbeing (Kudamatsu, 2012; Wang et al., 2018; Wigley & Akkoyunlu-Wigley, 2011). Political institutions affect decision-making (Hill & Leighley, 1992; Lijphart, 1997) because 'politicians and officials are under no compulsion to pay much heed to classes and groups of citizens that do not' get to participate in decision-making processes (Key & Heard, 1949). When political institutions systematically exclude some groups from decision-making, their health is likely to suffer because the concerns of excluded groups may be overlooked (Fowler, 2015; Geys,

2006; Krieger et al., 2014; Lijphart, 1997), even when those in power might be sympathetic to the policy preferences of the under-represented (Pontusson & Rueda, 2010). Put simply, political institutions govern who has voice and this may affect health. While a number of studies are beginning to document the health effects of political institutions (Bollyky et al., 2019; Wigley & Akkoyunlu-Wigley, 2011), this work is still in its infancy (Beckfield, 2018).

In this sense, patterns of health and disease are produced by the structures, values and priorities of political and economic systems (Krieger, 2001). Geographical patterns of health inequalities, at least in part, are shaped by the wider political, social and economic system and the actions of the state (government) and international level actors (Bambra, 2019). Politics and the balance of power between key political groups – notably labour and capital – determine the role of the state and other agencies in relation to health and whether there are collective interventions to improve health and reduce health inequalities, and also whether these interventions are individually, environmentally or structurally focused. In this way, politics (broadly understood) is the fundamental determinant of our health divides because it shapes the wider social, economic and physical environment and the social and spatial distribution of salutogenic and pathogenic factors both collectively and individually (Bambra, 2016).

5.5 Conclusion

This chapter has provided a brief overview of the different types of health inequalities that exist in all high-income countries and we have described some of the drivers of these inequalities in mortality and morbidity. The message of this chapter is straightforward: the politics of ageing is actually the politics of inequality. In other words, debates about the 'ageing crisis' could, in our estimation, be reframed as debates about health inequality. There are two reasons we hold this view.

Ageing is not a uniform process. Some adults live long and healthy lives and others do not. Many sadly never even get to reach 'old age', as defined by traditional metrics, while others suffer many years of pain and limited capacity as they live with chronic illnesses which constrain their ability to enjoy the kinds of lives they want to live. Unfortunately, such differences are not explained by luck alone. The substantial health inequalities that exist among the elderly are structured according to other inequalities in the social determinants of health. Differences in income, education and social background shape our everyday practices, such as whether we smoke or what we eat, and these affect our life chances. Beyond these individual characteristics, where we live can also alter the degree to which earning a good wage can protect our health. Earning a decent wage, for example, does not necessarily ensure access to good services. Our local communities can offset or enhance the other resources we have available to us as we pursue health and longevity.

One consequence of focusing on ageing specifically is that it seems to obfuscate the inequalities that are producing the ageing crisis. In other words, the ageing crisis – the prospect of many elderly people living longer lives – will be especially challenging if the inequalities in ageing become even greater, with many more people suffering poor health while living longer lives. Moreover, it seems to overlook that the foundation for the inequalities in ageing that we observe are actually laid at other points during the life-course. The work of life-course epidemiologists has repeatedly shown us that ageing trajectories are forged in childhood, adolescence and our working lives. Minimizing the fiscal risks associated with an ageing population requires a life-course approach.

In the next chapter we show that acknowledging that the politics of ageing is really the politics of inequality is crucial because the policy solutions that are sometimes proposed to address aspects of the ageing crisis are inherently linked with inequality. Indeed, in some cases they may very well exacerbate health inequalities, making the ageing crisis worse in the long run.

6 The Implications of Win-Win and Win-Lose Policies for the 'Ageing Crisis'

6.1 Introduction

The preceding chapters raise three issues that are crucial to understanding the politics of healthy ageing. First, older voters are not as powerful nor as unified as many politicians, think tanks and commentators often believe. While some elderly voters have preferences for policies that are in their own interests or in the interests of their children and grandchildren, older voters are not sufficiently homogeneous to act as a voting bloc. Indeed, even if they were, it is not clear that their influence on policy would be substantial because policy decisions are not simply determined by voters' demand. Second, in those few contexts where political conflict over policies is framed intergenerationally, the wellbeing of older people can be preserved without being at the expense of other groups, particularly those of working age. Reframing the debate in this way helps societies move from policies which individualize the responsibility of being healthy – by withdrawing government investment – to an emphasis on healthy ageing which seeks to establish cross-class/cross-generational coalitions. Third, inequalities in healthy ageing are structured according to other kinds of inequality in the social determinants of health, and these upstream inequalities are best understood when situated in a life-course perspective which recognizes that inequalities in ageing are the product of inequalities that manifest at much earlier stages in life. Not everybody gets to be old.

One implication that flows from this analysis is that the 'ageing crisis' and the political narrative that has gone along with it ('grey electoral power') has become so pervasive that it is altering the supply side of policy options. That is, when politicians, civil servants and think tanks begin to consider policy options within the constraints of the 'ageing crisis' narrative, then countries may become more likely to implement policies to protect older voters but which, ironically, undermine healthy ageing. This can happen even in countries where older people themselves are not necessarily advocating for these reforms. Rather, the discourse around these issues has become so pervasive that it creates the conditions in which 'win-lose' policies become more likely.

The argument of this chapter is that these 'win-lose' policies harm health among younger citizens and, in so doing, these same policies paradoxically contribute to the health problems of an ageing population. This is because ageing is not costly per se. Rather, getting older only increases costs if those older people are in poorer health. We illustrate the problem of win-lose policies in terms of improving healthy ageing via reducing health inequalities through exploring a series of case studies which illustrate the health effects of win-win or win-lose policies. To be clear, we are not arguing that these policies were implemented as a result of intergenerational conflict (this has been discussed in Chapters 3 and 4). Rather, we take examples of the kind of win-win and win-lose policies described in the introduction to illuminate how they affect health and healthy ageing.

6.2 Win-Win Policies and Healthy Ageing

Inequalities in health are not only pervasive, as we have discussed. They also seem remarkably durable (Mackenbach, 2017; Reeves, 2017b). Indeed, one of the key debates in public health and allied fields is whether achieving reductions in health inequalities is possible through government intervention. This debate has crucial implications for inequalities in healthy ageing and whether win-win policies could minimize the economic risks associated with the ageing crisis. One of the great disappointments of public health is that health inequalities seem to persist in high-income countries despite substantial improvement in living standards, the creation of welfare states and concerted government efforts to reduce such disparities (Hu et al., 2016; Mackenbach, 2012). Professor Johan Mackenbach has, in recent years, struck a more pessimistic note than many in the field, arguing that 'reducing health inequalities is currently beyond our means' (Mackenbach, 2010). Many do not agree with him, however. Professor Sir Michael Marmot, for example, is far more optimistic. His recent book lays out the evidence behind health gaps around the world but it also argues that these inequalities are not only avoidable but that 'we know what to do to make a difference' to health inequalities (Marmot, 2015). In other words, societies can address inequalities in healthy ageing and they know how to do it – they just need the political will to do so (Bambra, 2016). This does not mean that reducing health inequalities across the life-course is straightforward, but this section examines two examples of how health inequalities have been successfully reduced through policies which embody 'win-win' approaches to the ageing crisis. We begin with the English health inequalities strategy (2000–2010) and then turn to a rather unusual example of win-win policies by examining Germany post-Reunification (1990–2010) in order to draw lessons for other European countries.

6.2.1 The English Health Inequalities Strategy as a Win-Win Strategy

In 1997 a Labour government was elected in England on a manifesto that included a commitment to reducing health inequalities. This led to the implementation between 2000 and 2010 of a wide-ranging and multi-faceted health inequalities reduction strategy for England (Mackenbach, 2010) in which policymakers systematically and explicitly attempted to reduce inequalities in health. The strategy focused specifically on supporting families, engaging communities in tackling deprivation, improving prevention, increasing access to health care and tackling the underlying social determinants of health (Mackenbach, 2010). For example, the strategy included large increases in levels of public spending on a range of social programmes, the introduction of the national minimum wage, area-based interventions such as the Health Action Zones and a substantial increase in expenditure on the health care system (Robinson et al., 2019). The latter was targeted at more deprived neighbourhoods when, after 2002, a 'health inequalities weighting' was added to the way in which National Health Service (NHS) funds were geographically distributed, so that areas of higher deprivation received more funds per head to reflect higher health need (Bambra, 2016). Furthermore, the government also made tackling health, social and educational inequalities a public service priority by setting public service agreement targets. The key targets of the Labour government's health inequalities strategy were to: (1) reduce the gap in life expectancy at birth between the most deprived local authorities and the English average by 10 per cent by 2010; and (2) cut inequalities in the infant mortality rate by 10 per cent by 2010.

Part of Mackenbach's scepticism was rooted in an early analysis of England's efforts to reduce health inequalities following the election of New Labour in 1997. Those papers suggested the strategy had not delivered the expected results (Hu et al., 2016), concluding 'if this did not work, what will'? (Mackenbach, 2010). However, more recent empirical examinations of this investment has suggested that these reforms did reduce inequalities, at least geographical inequalities in health (Barr et al., 2014; Barr et al., 2017; Buck & Maguire, 2015; Robinson et al., 2019). What is particularly striking about these analyses is that they suggest the reversal of these policies, which largely occurred following the implementation of austerity in the UK, actually stopped progress towards reducing health inequalities and may have even led to them increasing.

Recent empirical studies have found that the strategy was partially effective. Barr et al. (2017) found that geographical inequalities in life expectancy declined during the English health inequalities strategy period, reversing a previously increasing trend. Before the strategy, the gap in life expectancy between the most deprived local authorities in England and the rest of the country increased at a rate of 0.57 months each year for men and 0.30 months each year for women. During the strategy period this trend reversed, and the gap in life expectancy for men declined by 0.91 months each year and for women by 0.50 months each year. Barr et al. (2017) also found that since the end of the strategy period the inequality gap has increased again at a rate of 0.68 months each year for men and 0.31 months each year for women. At the end of the English health inequalities strategy period, the gap in male life expectancy was 1.2 years smaller and the gap in female life expectancy was 0.6 years smaller than would have been the case if the trends in inequalities before the strategy had continued.

Further, Robinson et al. (2019) investigated whether the English health inequalities strategy was associated with a decrease in geographical inequalities in infant mortality rate. They found that before New Labour's health inequalities strategy (1983–98), the gap in the infant mortality rate between the most deprived local authorities and the rest of England increased at a rate of 3 infant deaths per 100,000 births per year. During the strategy period (1999–2010) the gap narrowed by 12 infant deaths per 100,000 births per year and after the strategy period ended (2011–17) the gap began increasing again at a rate of 4 deaths per 100,000 births per year. This is shown in Figure 6.1.

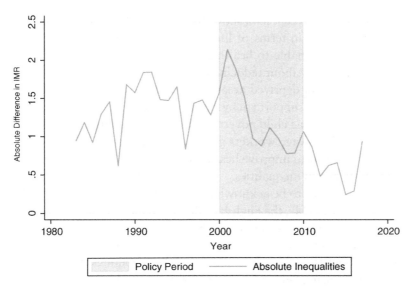

Figure 6.1 Trends in absolute inequalities in infant mortality rate (IMR), 20 per cent most deprived local authorities compared to the rest of England, 1983 to 2017.

Source: adapted from Robinson et al., 2019, with permission from BMJ Publishing

Another area of strategy success was around reducing geographical inequalities in mortality amenable to health care, which is defined as mortality from causes for which there is evidence that they can be prevented given timely and appropriate access to high quality care (Nolte & McKee, 2011). NHS funding was increased from 2001 when the aforementioned 'health inequalities weighting' was added to the way in which NHS funds were geographically distributed to target funding to areas of higher deprivation. Analysis has shown that this policy of increasing the proportion of resources allocated to deprived areas as compared to more affluent areas was associated with a reduction in absolute health inequalities from causes amenable to health care (Barr et al., 2014). Increases in NHS resources to deprived areas accounted for a reduction in the gap between deprived and affluent areas in male 'mortality amenable to health care' of 35 deaths per 100,000 and female mortality of 16 deaths per 100,000. Each additional £10 million of resources allocated to deprived areas was associated with a reduction in 4 male deaths per 100,000 and 2 female deaths per 100,000 (Barr et al., 2014).

Thus, the most recent data show that the English strategy did reduce health inequalities in terms of life expectancy, infant mortality rates and mortality amenable to health care. So, what does New Labour's experience teach us about reducing health inequalities? First, investing in good services in deprived areas (Barr et al., 2017), the creation of programmes which support young families, such as Sure Start (Sammons et al., 2015), reducing child poverty whilst protecting older households, and ensuring low-wage workers get paid a decent wage (Reeves et al., 2017a) all seemed to improve health and may have contributed to the reduction in health inequalities.

However, it has to be acknowledged that the decreases were on the modest side. Arguably, the English health inequalities strategy may have been even more effective in reducing health inequalities if there had not been a gradual 'lifestyle drift' in governance – whereby policy went from thinking about the social determinants of health alongside behaviour change, to focusing almost exclusively on individual behaviour change (Whitehead & Popay, 2010). Only so much can be achieved in terms of reducing health inequalities by focusing only on individual-level behaviour change (a form of 'win-lose' policy) or the provision of treatment services such as smoking cessation programmes or by increasing access to health care services. There is a need to also address the more fundamental social and economic causes. Whilst some policies enacted under the 1997–2010 Labour governments focused on the more fundamental determinants (e.g. the implementation of a national minimum wage, the minimum pension, tax credits for working parents, and a reduction in child poverty), as well as significant investment in the health care system, there was, however, little substantial redistribution of income between rich and poor (Lynch, 2020). Nor was there much by way of an economic rebalancing of the country (e.g. between north and south). Further, in wider policy areas the Labour governments continued the neoliberal approach of Thatcherism, including, for example, further marketization and privatization of the health care system (Scott-Samuel et al., 2014). The strategy may also have been even more effective if it had been sustained over a longer time period. But the global financial crisis of 2007–8 led to the premature end of the English health inequalities strategy, a change of governing political party and an increase again in health inequalities (Taylor-Robinson et al., 2019).

So, the lessons we learn from England's strategy are only relevant to a particular vision of what society could be. The Labour governments of 1997–2010 did not fundamentally try to alter the political economy of society but rather to harness the two impulses of both neoliberalism and progressive politics. Their approach was to 'let the market rip' and then use taxes and transfers to redistribute wealth to those communities not benefiting from the explosion of growth (Lynch, 2020). They did not attempt to pursue more radical policies that would fundamentally reorganize society, for example by shifting the mode of capitalism that dominates within the UK (Hall & Soskice, 2001). It is, of course, very difficult to make such radical leaps from one type of political economy to another, as economic and political institutions are path dependent (Beramendi et al., 2015). But what Labour's experience cannot tell us is what would have happened had they tried to do so. This is, in fact, where Mackenbach's basic pessimism comes from: he is profoundly sceptical that such radical breaks from one political-economic arrangement to another are politically feasible. However, this does overlook the emergence of powerful narratives that have enabled countries to embark on radical reforms that reduced inequality – such as in post-war Britain and Europe with the setting-up of the welfare state and free, universal health care (Scheve & Stasavage, 2016).

6.2.2 German Reunification: Drawing Lessons from an Unusual Win-Win

There is another dimension to debates about what will work to improve healthy ageing and reduce health inequalities that it is important to stress, and that is the issue of time. Mackenbach is also attuned to this when he acknowledges that health inequalities are the result of the cumulative impact of decades of exposure to health risks, some of them intergenerational, of those who live in socioeconomically less advantaged circumstances (Mackenbach, 2010). Inequalities within age-groups, including among the elderly, are not solely the product of current practices and a contemporary socioeconomic position. Rather, habits of consumption over many years both reflect and interact with exposure to sustained economic conditions that structure our lives to generate health inequalities (Bartley, 2016).

This comes through in life-course research which has repeatedly observed that the conditions into which children are born and then raised cast a long shadow over their health for the rest of their lives (Ben-Shlomo & Kuh, 2002). Children born into lower socioeconomic positions have poorer physical capabilities in later years; for example, they have slower walking speeds and find it more difficult to get out of a chair (Birnie et al., 2011). While such reduced mobility is a negative health outcome in and of itself, these measures are also highly predictive of future mortality rates too (Kuh et al., 2014). Birth weight is positively related to grip strength (Kuh et al., 2014) and grip strength also predicts mortality (Celis-Morales et al., 2018). Crucially, birth weight is influenced by the generosity of the welfare state (Strully et al., 2010).

This is not just about childhood. Living in poor quality housing for many years has an additional negative impact on your health over and above the influence of living in poor quality housing today (Pevalin et al., 2017). Neighbourhoods too have a scarring effect on health. Living in a deprived neighbourhood during your adult life increases your allostatic load in adulthood, even after accounting for your own personal living conditions (Gustafsson et al., 2014).

As Professor Ted Schrecker has argued, addressing health inequalities will require a substantial redistribution of resources, but it will also require time (Schrecker, 2017). The example of German Reunification provides an example of reductions in regional health inequalities over a twenty-year period. In 1989 – before the fall of the Berlin Wall – there was a four year life expectancy gap between East and West Germany. But this East-West gap rapidly narrowed in the following decades so that by 2010 it had dwindled to just a few months for women and just over six months for men (Figures 6.2 and 6.3) (Bambra et al., 2014; Bambra, 2016). So, how was this done?

First, the living standards of East Germans improved with the economic terms of the Reunification whereby the West German Deutsche Mark (a strong internationally traded currency) replaced the East German Mark (considered almost worthless outside of the Eastern bloc) as the official currency – a Mark for a Mark. This meant that salaries and savings were replaced equally, one to one, by the much higher value Deutsche Mark. Substantial investment was also made into the industries of Eastern Germany and transfer payments were made by the West German government to ensure the future funding of social welfare programmes in the East. This meant that by as early as 1996, wages in the East rose very rapidly to around 75 per cent of Western levels from being less than 40 per cent in 1990 (Kibele et al., 2015). This increase in incomes was also experienced by old age pensioners. In 1985 retired households in the East had only 36 per cent of the income of employed

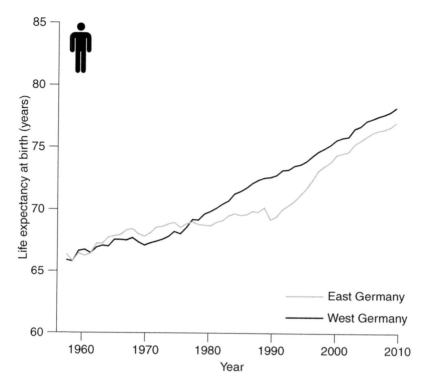

Figure 6.2 Trends in male life expectancy in Former East and West Germany to 2010.

Source: reproduced from Bambra, 2016, with permission of Policy Press

households, whilst retirees in the West received 65 per cent (Gjonca et al., 2000). After Reunification the West German pension system was extended into the East which resulted in huge increases in income for older East Germans: in 1990 the monthly pension of an East German pensioner was only 40 per cent of that a Western pensioner, but by 1999 it had increased to 87 per cent of West German levels (Gjonca et al., 2000). This meant that retired people were one of the groups that benefited most from Reunification, particularly East German women as they had, on average, considerably longer working biographies than their West German counterparts (Gjonca et al., 2000).

Secondly, access to a variety of foods and consumer goods also increased as West German shops and companies set up in the East. It has been argued that this led to decreases in cardiovascular diseases as

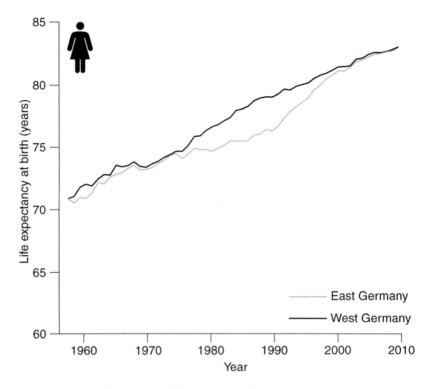

Figure 6.3 Trends in female life expectancy in Former East and West Germany to 2010.

Source: Reproduced from Bambra, 2016, with permission of Policy Press

a result of better diets (Nolte et al., 2002). It was not all Keynesianism for the 'Ossis' (Easterners), though, as unemployment (unheard of in the full employment socialist system) also increased as a result of the rapid privatization and de-industrialization of the Eastern economy and, indeed, unemployment still remains nearly double that of the West today. A special solidarity surcharge had, however, been introduced to fund economic improvements. This was levied at a rate of up to 5.5 per cent on income taxes owed across both East and West (e.g. a tax bill of €5,000 attracts a solidarity surcharge of €275) (Gokhale et al., 1994).

Thirdly, immediately after Reunification considerable financial support was given to modernize the hospitals and health care equipment in the East, and the availability of nursing care, screening and pharmaceuticals also increased. This raised standards of health care in the East so that they were comparable to those of the West within just a few years (Nolte et al., 2002). This had notable impacts on neonatal mortality rates and falling death rates from conditions amenable to primary prevention or medical treatment (Nolte et al., 2002).

Both the economic reforms and the increased investment in health care were the result of the deep and sustained political decision to reunify Germany as fully as possible so that, as Chancellor Kohl stated, 'what belongs together will grow together'. Germany's lessons for reducing health inequalities and reducing unequal ageing are therefore two-fold: firstly, even large health inequalities can be significantly reduced, over time; secondly, the tools to do this are largely economic but – crucially – within the control of politics and politicians. Ultimately, the German experience shows that if there is sufficient political desire to reduce unequal ageing, it can be done. It shows the primacy of politics and economics, underlying the need for a political dimension to our understanding of how to reduce health inequalities.

And yet, despite the case study evidence in favour of investing in social protection and creating institutions which ensure a more equitable distribution of both wealth and opportunity, there are reasons to be cautious about simply extrapolating from these two country case studies. The same intervention will not work the same everywhere because it will inevitably interact with pre-existing conditions and attitudes, and the outcomes are not straightforwardly predictable. We certainly have some good evidence that particular reforms have improved (or aggravated) health inequalities in some contexts, but what is less clear is whether we can take those reforms to other countries and deliver the same results.

6.3 Win-Lose Policies and the Implications for Healthy Ageing

Win-win policies may reduce health inequalities, but this does not necessarily mean that win-lose policies make them any worse. This is in part because the distinction between high- and win-lose is not necessarily just a question of 'treatment' intensity and so we cannot think about the association between government policy and health inequalities as a simple dose-response relationship. In part, this is because there are likely to be all kinds of non-linearities and spill-over effects which will play out differently in win-win and win-lose contexts. Indeed, if win-win contexts are places where policies are coherently pulling towards a life-course approach to ensuring healthy ageing, then win-lose contexts may be precisely the kinds of places where incoherent policies are pulling in different directions and thereby make some inequalities worse but others better, with little overall change in general population. In these win-lose settings, the marginal influence of government may simply be quite small. Of course, if Marmot is right – that health inequalities are avoidable and we know how to avoid them – then win-lose policies may indeed exacerbate the gaps in health outcomes between the privileged and the deprived. This section again explores these issues through two 'win-lose' policy case studies: austerity in the UK and the Americanization of European economies. Both of them are rooted in liberal market economies in part because these are places where win-lose policies have been implemented but also because these are sites where politicians have perceived the electoral power of older votes to be large (even if in practical terms it has not been as substantial as many might have thought). These cases are examples of countries where win-lose policies have been pursued in light of – albeit perhaps not directly caused by – the narrative around the ageing crisis.

6.3.1 Austerity Politics and Ageing in the UK

We start again with the UK because it is such a crucial case. Not only is the UK an example of an attempt to pursue win-win policies, but the pursuit of austerity policies over the last decade (2010–20) provides some hints at how failing to take the win-win may create long-term health challenges that could affect the ageing process. Stagnating life expectancy in the UK, for example, has been driven by a mix of rising mortality among both the elderly and, more surprisingly, those of working age (PHE, 2018). Perhaps more striking, inequalities in life expectancy have tragically risen in the last few years, according to recently released figures from the Office for National Statistics (ONS, 2019). There are also signs that inequalities in infant mortality rates may also be increasing – particularly in areas that have experienced the greatest increases in child poverty (Taylor-Robinson et al., 2019). This is not only because of greater improvements among the better-off but because the poorest have also experienced real declines. In the most deprived parts of England, female life expectancy at birth fell by almost 100 days between 2012 and 2017. Men in the poorest areas saw no improvements while those in the richest parts of the UK continued to see their life expectancies improve. This will have implications for inequalities in ageing into the future.

Given our arguments above, falling life expectancy is not entirely unexpected. Indeed, part of the explanation of these unprecedented changes may be rooted in economic reforms implemented in the UK since the economic crisis. As a political response to the 2007–8 financial crisis, the 2010 Conservative-led coalition government pursued a policy of austerity, characterized by a drive to reduce public deficits via large-scale cuts to central and local government budgets, reduced funding for the health care system, and large reductions in welfare services and working-age social security benefits. These changes appear to be increasingly linked to rising geographical inequalities and health inequalities (Pearce, 2013). While the government boasted about record levels of employment, we have seen the quality of work and wage levels decline. The number of children living in absolute poverty rose by 200,000 between 2016–17 and 2017–18, and risks hitting record levels (Richardson, 2019). In-work poverty continues to rise. The proportion of poor who live in working households has never been higher (70 per cent), and the face of poverty is getting younger too: 53 per cent of poor children are under the age of 5. Living standards actually fell last year. This is not remotely normal; it means families have been left struggling to afford to heat their homes, feed their families and even access health care (Loopstra et al., 2015; Reeves et al., 2015).

Austerity has been central to these changes. Cuts to housing benefit have meant households have not been able to respond to the rising cost of housing and the benefits freeze has slowly undermined the generosity of social security payments (Barnard, 2019; Reeves et al., 2016). The punitive sanction regime and the draconian implementation of working capability assessments have both created destitution, pushed people onto antidepressants and may have even induced higher suicide rates (Barr et al., 2016; Loopstra et al., 2018).

Take the benefits freeze. Since 2016 the value of social security payments has been fixed at 2015 prices. This freeze has affected more than 27 million people, and swept around 400,000 into poverty (Barnard, 2019). Unable to deal with the rising tide of higher prices, low-income families are, on average, £340 a year worse off than they would have been. This has been one of the costliest aspects of austerity, but we are only just starting to see the effects of this change in health data because the latest figures on inequalities in life expectancy come from 2015–17, the very start of the freeze.

Alongside the benefits freeze, we are still in the middle of the roll-out of Universal Credit. The Work and Pensions Committee have pointed out 'fundamental flaw[s] in the benefit's design' which may lead to a 'human and political catastrophe' (Keen et al., 2017). Emerging evidence suggests Universal Credit has created homelessness, hunger and destitution (Hay, 2019; Jitendra et al., 2018). Moreover, we are still waiting for the most significant change, bringing all current recipients of tax credits onto the programme (~7 million people in total when it is complete) (Hills, 2014). Particularly concerning is the high rate of sanctions faced by those on Universal Credit (up to 7 per cent of claimants every month). When sanctions were deployed at high rates under the Job Seekers Allowance, it merely pushed people away from the labour market, leaving them to rely on informal forms of support (Loopstra et al., 2015; NAO, 2016; Reeves, 2017a).

The UK's austerity measures tended to focus on people of working age, leaving pensioners in a better position than ever, through a series of reforms that ensured growth in the value of the state pension (Akhter et al., 2018). But the elderly were not protected in every country. Due to population ageing, pensions have become one of the largest single areas of public expenditure in high-income countries. It is unsurprising therefore that governments around Europe used this moment to reconfigure pension schemes to cut spending on the elderly. Shortly after austerity began to spread, the OECD expressed concern that proposed cuts to pensions would only harm the financial security of the elderly. Many countries went ahead anyway: Czechia and Norway altered indexation rules to reduce spending over the long term, while Greece and Hungary took a more immediate approach, implementing fairly stark reductions in the value of payments. These changes have not been benign either, and have led to increases in unmet medical need among the elderly, particularly for those who were already at the bottom of the income distribution. Reductions in European state pensions have widened inequalities in access to social care, and this may be partially behind the excessive fatalities amongst most deprived groups linked to the coronavirus epidemic that has ravaged elderly populations across the continent (see Chapter 5, Section 2.7).

In the area of health care, Britain's approach to the NHS provides an intriguing case. It did not increase co-payments but neither did it expand services. Instead, spending on health was 'ring-fenced' by the Conservative-led coalition government, and this in the context of major reductions in spending almost everywhere else. And yet, this ring-fence created the most sustained decline ever in NHS spending as a percentage of GDP, simultaneously producing the most financially difficult decade for the NHS since its inception. American political scientist Jacob Hacker calls such changes 'policy drift', when the maintenance of the status quo slowly stops it from adapting to shifting social conditions and changing risks. Over the last few winters the NHS has increasingly struggled to cope with the demands placed upon it. The coronavirus pandemic has provided a stark example of how long-term underfunding has impacted on the health care system, with all health care providers cancelling all non-essential surgeries, leading to immense backlogs and waiting lists, and arguably contributing to excess non-coronavirus deaths – especially in more deprived neighbourhoods (Bambra et al., 2020; Bambra et al., 2021). Subsequently, the mortality rate in the first quarter of 2018 was the highest since 2009.

Elderly people are one of the groups most reliant on effective health and social care services. When these services break down, the elderly will suffer, and these data suggest that some of the most vulnerable – that is, the oldest old – have indeed been left exposed. These real-term reductions in public expenditure on social care associated with austerity policies in the UK were associated with higher mortality rates among the elderly, especially those in care homes – precisely those groups who seem to be driving the slow-down in improvements in life expectancy in the UK. This is especially tragic because a muddled plan to address the deficit in social care spending during the 2015 UK general election missed an opportunity to address this crisis, leaving many elderly people exposed to inadequate social care and, all too often, shorter lives – especially given the particular vulnerability of the over-80s to respiratory conditions, including the coronavirus pandemic.

Austerity is a 'slow train coming'; an unfolding crisis that is only now becoming visible in the published data, and it is interacting with and exacerbating the impacts of the coronavirus pandemic (Bambra et al., 2020). The true impact of austerity goes well beyond the most immediate health consequences because of its impact on material deprivation driven by cuts to social protection and other social services, including health systems. Poverty harms health, but the implications may not manifest themselves in the same year or even in the year after. Poverty has a scarring effect on health, but it may take some time for these scarring effects to show up as higher rates of mortality. In part, this is because austerity has powerful supporters. Many countries are still waiting to implement, or at least implement fully, austerity measures announced some years ago. The restructuring of welfare states in response to the 2007–8 global financial crisis and now the coronavirus economic depression is ongoing.

6.3.2 Health Inequalities and the "Americanization" of European Political Economy

Stalling life expectancy in Europe is closely linked with higher mortality among the elderly, while in the USA rising mortality rates have been most striking among people of working age (Case & Deaton, 2015). Unsurprisingly, the causes of death have been quite different too, mainly suicides and drug overdoses in the USA – what Case and Deaton call 'deaths of despair' (Case & Deaton, 2015). Many of these deaths are clearly not the product of the Great Recession alone, nor of any systematic state retrenchment in response to the financial crisis. With austerity, European countries are, in many instances, merely emulating the neoliberal economic and welfare reforms already implemented in the USA in the 1980s and 1990s, which also reduced the generosity of welfare and increased conditionality. European countries such as the UK and Germany are now witnessing stagnating wages, something Americans have lived with for almost thirty years. So, what are the implications of the Americanization of European political, welfare and economic systems for the future of healthy ageing?

It is well established that the USA has a significant mortality disadvantage relative to other wealthy countries – with, for example, life expectancy rates that are more than three years less than France and Sweden (Avendano & Kawachi, 2014) and growing mortality and morbidity rates, particularly amongst middle-aged, low income Whites (Case & Deaton, 2015). It also has higher health inequalities – particularly in terms of ethnicity and income (Bambra, 2019). These can be explained through the political economy of the USA.

One political economy mechanism behind the worse health of the USA is through the relatively limited regulation of unhealthy products, such as tobacco, alcohol and ultra-processed food and drinks, and the industries that produce and market these products (Freudenberg, 2016). The USA is one of the least regulated markets among high income countries, and is one of only a small number of high income countries not to have ratified the Framework Convention on Tobacco Control (WHOon, 2003). These various political and economic factors interact to shape the health of Americans unevenly, contributing to the country's extensive health inequalities (Krieger et al., 2014). Geographical work has shown that tobacco, alcohol and ultra-processed foods tend to be highly available in low income urban areas of the USA, and that the products are increasingly targeted at, and available to, low income and minority populations – thereby shaping the local context within which health inequalities arise (Beaulac et al., 2009).

A second mechanism is through higher rates of poverty in the USA compared to most of Europe. The state provision of social welfare is minimal in the USA, with modest social insurance benefits which are often regulated via strict entitlement criteria, with recipients often being subject to means-testing and receipt, accordingly, being stigmatized (Bambra, 2016). This is particularly the case in health care, where even after the implementation of the Affordable Care Act health insurance and access to care remained politically contentious and deficient for many. This contributed to declining life expectancy (US National Academy of Medicine, 2021). The USA now provides the lowest level of welfare generosity and the lowest level of health care access of high income democracies (Bambra, 2016). Indeed, the relative underperformance of the US social security system has been associated with a reduction of up to four years in life expectancy at the population level (Beckfield & Bambra, 2016).

Thirdly, internationally, collective bargaining and political incorporation have also been associated with national health outcomes. Countries with higher rates of trade union membership have more extensive welfare systems and higher levels of income redistribution – and correspondingly have lower rates of income inequality (Pickett & Wilkinson, 2010). They also have better health and safety regulations. The USA long had the lowest rate of trade union membership amongst wealthy democracies, restricting the representation of working class interests in policy and politics. For example, in 2010 only 12 per cent of the workforce in the USA was a member of a trade union. In contrast, the rates were 26 per cent in the UK and 68 per cent in Sweden (Schrecker & Bambra, 2015). Further, the political incorporation of minority groups is also robustly associated with better health among those groups, suggesting a direct connection between political empowerment and health (Krieger & Ruhose, 2013). The USA was a historical laggard in terms of the incorporation of minority groups – with equal civil rights for African-Americans only achieved in the 1960s (Krieger & Ruhose, 2013).

The combination of all of these political and economic factors helps to explain why the US has a mortality disadvantage relative to other countries and why it has become more pronounced since 1980 (when neoliberal economics led to welfare retrenchment, de-industrialization and deregulation) (Schrecker & Bambra, 2015), arguably leading to the increasing mortality and morbidity rates amongst middle-aged, low income Whites that are now being observed (Navarro, 2019). By exporting neoliberal policies (e.g. through political/policy transfer and/or trade agreements) that keep wages low and earnings insecure, particularly for those with less education, the USA may also be exporting the conditions which have created 'deaths of despair' and increased health inequalities in the USA. Europe may never reach the levels seen in the USA due to differences in the political economy of European health care systems, but the USA may provide a grim forecast of what future European health and ageing crises may look like if Europe also fosters an environment where there is a steady deterioration in economic and social opportunities. This is increasingly a pressing issue in light of the severe economic recession that has followed the coronavirus crisis.

6.4 Conclusion

This chapter has argued that 'win-lose' policy choices – policies that are now often discursively framed and advocated in Europe partly as a solution to the ageing crisis – can produce health inequalities across the life-course because they fail to recognize that the cost of ageing today is rooted in health inequalities created in the recent past. Greater health inequalities in the early years will not simply disappear by the time people reach older ages and it is these inequalities in healthy ageing that are the real cost to society. Indeed, policies that deepen inequalities in health among younger groups in order to protect the assumed interests and economic power of older voters are merely exacerbating the future costs of an unequal, ageing population. This has been shown in a devastating manner in relation to the coronavirus pandemic, where countries with a higher burden of chronic disease amongst the elderly have had higher mortality rates. The politics of intergenerational conflict is really after all the politics of inequality.

This politics of intergenerational conflict is not inevitable, however. Our analysis has revealed examples of 'win-win' political choices that governments can make to reduce current and future health inequalities – by expanding the social safety net. The solidarity shown across generations in relation to the coronavirus pandemic also gives reason for optimism. We have also shown how 'win-lose' policies of austerity and neoliberalism are resulting in increased health inequalities by reducing the social safety net – arguably storing up problems for healthy ageing in the future. This does not mean that such choices are easy. Certainly the path dependence of countries' political and economic institutions make it hard to simply shift towards health investments across the life-course, especially in settings where tax rises could be unpopular (Lynch, 2020). But, as Chapter 3 shows, it is possible to build coalitions – particularly when key socio-demographic groups such as women and unions are effectively mobilized – that promote healthy ageing for all and in the process address the financial burdens imposed through an ageing population.

Acknowledgements

Sections of this chapter are based on Clare Bambra (2016) *Health Divides: Where You Live Can Kill You*, adapted and reproduced with permission of the author and Policy Press. Clare Bambra is a senior investigator in CHAIN: Centre for Global Health Inequalities Research (Norwegian Research Council project number 288638).

7 | Conclusion

This book has, we hope, destroyed two straw men that are common in debates about intergenerational equity, spending and health. The first is the myth of 'greedy geezers' – the stereotype of a pampered pensioner, living off lavish old-age provision including fine health care, while voting against investments in future generations. The second is the myth of unsustainability – of health care costs driven by ageing that make it impossible to finance a welfare state. The two straw men arguments come together in a call for cuts to public health care and other public service provision: the former by demonizing older people, the latter by suggesting that public provision, unlike private finance, is unsustainable. The images of greedy older people and an ineluctably increasing financial burden associated with ageing both strengthen the argument against public provision.

The economics and health system analysis behind this argument is weak. An ageing society need not affect health care much. In fact, as we suggested in the Introduction, there is no meaningful question about the best policy or priority that is answered by focusing on ageing. Obviously, planning long-term care or developing the health workforce or designing accessible spaces are activities in which demographic change matters, but they are properly understood as relatively technical problems that can be solved without major political change. Claims that policy or politics inexorably leads to a clash of generations are simply wrong, belied by policy analysis, political practice and the behaviour of people.

Instead, it is possible to envision both win-win policies and win-win politics. Win-win policies are those which invest in people across the life-cycle, avoiding false choices by targeting the conditions of health and wellbeing at any age. Win-win politics, meanwhile, simply avoid assuming that there is a zero-sum conflict between generations, which is easy because in neither health policy nor electoral behaviour does any such conflict necessarily exist. The origin of zero-sum, win-lose, politics lies in elite and interest group coalitions that furnish the supply of political ideas. This chapter recaps the reasons why win-lose politics need not happen and make a poor descriptive theory of ageing politics, and then argues for a focus on broad public policies that can create win-win or win-lose policies.

7.1 Tearing Down Straw Men

So why are the straw men made of straw? The first and simplest reason why is that we all age, and in fact are doing so every day. That means age cannot be a stable political cleavage. While marketers have done wonders to persuade the media that generations have stable characteristics (boomers, Generation X, Millennials, etc.), there is little evidence of that. Meanwhile, families redistribute resources across generations, tying people together and redefining their interests in ways that extend people's time horizons and draw upon better motivations than simple avarice.

The second reason is that older people are heterogeneous. There is heterogeneity *between countries*. Put simply, the narrative of greedy pensioners sunning themselves in the Mediterranean is very much a Western European one. It is a nonsensical idea for much of Central and Eastern Europe, where poverty among the elderly is a serious issue and the scale of unmet health needs suggests that health services are not disproportionately catering to them. Even between rich Western European states there is considerable heterogeneity. The experience of older people, their health status and use of health care, and their financial situation are all quite different from country to country. Even getting to be old at all varies and is substantially predicted by other, well-known inequalities such as income, place and race. The relatively inflamed intergenerational politics of the UK and USA, however influential they may be in English-language debates, are an outlier and not a harbinger.

There is also heterogeneity *within countries*. One of the most alarming findings we present is that there is a positive relationship between inter- and intragenerational inequality: countries with overall social spending more skewed towards the elderly are the ones with more inequality among the elderly. The countries with the most rhetoric about the unjustly good lifestyle of pensioners, and the most striking flow of public resources to the over-65s, are precisely the countries with the most pensioner poverty.

The third reason the straw men are made of straw is that the whole argument about greedy older people depends on a popular model of politics that good political science will not sustain. To claim that a large bloc of older voters is shaping public policy to their tastes, against the interest of others, is to claim that (1) older voters have homogeneous interests shaped by their age as against other issues such as wealth, gender or labour market position; (2) that they vote on these interests; and (3) that politicians deliver policies in response to their interests. None of these three assertions has strong empirical justification. There is no reason to believe, and no evidence, that political identities and policy preferences are primarily shaped by age. Not only are political identities much more complex and citizens often uninterested in much policy, but ageing itself means different things for the sicker, healthier, richer, poorer, etc. Even when people think about age, they are likely to personalize it and think about their families, which span generations. Selfishness is not just hard to translate into concrete policy, it is not even all that demonstrably popular.

The reason is even more important for understanding politics: there is little reason to believe in the underlying demand-side model of politics in which politicians identify the preferences of the electorate and then cater to them (Gilens, 2012; Hacker & Pierson, 2014; Mair, 2013)[1]. Far superior are models in which politics happens at the level of elites such as party leaders, major interest groups and policy entrepreneurs. Their interaction, which can be understood in a variety of established political science theories, produce the 'supply' of policy demands and shape the political agenda including the salience and content of debates about health care and ageing. Voters do not formulate their own lists of policy demands and ask politicians to deliver them; rather, politicians develop policy 'offers' that balance their electoral interests against other issues such as coalitional politics amongst elites, and constraints such as fiscal pressure. Satisfying coalitional allies and bond markets, making targeted electoral offers and managing relations with other politicians are all much more concrete, observable and powerful explanations of political activity than a search for the mythical demands of a mythical

---

[1] These are median voter models, akin to representative agent thinking in economics, in which politicians are assumed to cater to the interests of the median voter, a fictitious creature whose existence depends on the assumption that voters are neatly aligned on a single axis with a median. The attraction of this model is not in its realism or usefulness, but in the way it can convert the entire electorate into a single agent (the median voter), and posit a gravitational pull towards centrist policy.

and remarkably policy-literate median voter. They also fit with the fact that there is no single axis on which voters easily align; politicians and the media can change the subject, elevating topics which work for their interests and repressing inconvenient ones (thus, for example, making immigration and crime more prominent on the agenda is often an explicit strategy of parties on the right that benefit when the attention is there). Put another way: if polling data or median voters drove politics, the USA would have universal and equitable health care access and most countries would have universal jobs guarantees.

7.2 Equity, Intergenerational and Other

Political elites are expert in changing the subject. When *any* policy argument puts the spotlight on one issue, we should ask what is being left in the dark. In the case of a focus on the politics of ageing and health, the price of a focus on intergenerational inequality is a loss of focus on almost every other dimension of inequality. It is not hard to see why people whose policy goal is to shrink public health care provision and expose more people to the market would want to foment intergenerational conflict. What if we do not listen to them, and instead ask what other kinds of inequality are at work, shaping life chances and the politics of ageing?

There are many. *Racial and ethnic* inequalities shape life chances and, in the context of the politics of ageing, also shape the likelihood that people at any stage of the life-course are helped or helping, for free or for often inadequate pay. *Citizenship* exacerbates these inequalities, since one way to reduce the cost of care is to exploit undocumented people or others with precarious citizenship. *Gender* inequalities are enormous in the context of ageing, since the preponderance of paid and unpaid care is delivered by women, with consequences for their own health, wellbeing and labour market status. Above all, *income and wealth* inequalities are at work. The stronger and more universal the public provision, the less it matters how much money a family has, and the less likely it is that costs associated with ageing fall upon a family in a way that does real damage. This is important because a family's wealth, in particular, can be wiped out by the costs of long-term care. Resetting the inheritance of many families to zero every generation in order to pay for long-term care should have effects on long-term mobility and stability.

Chapters 5 and 6 approached this issue, urging us to keep our eye on the much larger issues obscured by a focus on ageing, in particular the inequalities and equity issues that, unlike generations, do actually matter. When we put the spotlight on generations, we illuminate very little at the price of obscuring the important issues.

7.3 After the Straw Men: Understanding the Politics of Ageing and Health

Other inequalities and heterogeneity shape political identities, politics and policies more than generations. Policies matter in shaping the interaction of ageing with those other, more consequential, inequalities. Much of the evidence is in how much states matter: the scale of interstate heterogeneity in cross-section. A place like the Belgian-French-Luxembourg-Netherlands border region might look integrated and relatively undifferentiated, but the lives of citizens at every age are quite different on different sides of those likes.

Much evidence is also in change, and that is most promising for our analyses. Policy and political change are constant, and create constantly changing opportunities as well as constraints on political creativity. Chapter 4 focused on change as well as interstate differences. It finds some constants: benefits to the aged hold up under austerity better than other kinds of benefits, presumably because of the political, human and other costs of reducing benefits to people who have left the labour market and are unlikely to return. But changes are also interesting: under what circumstances do win-win solutions appear?

From this perspective, creating and mobilizing intergenerational conflict is a political and policy strategy. The simple strategy, much discussed in the pensions literature, is to cut future pensions by leaving pension entitlements alone for current pensioners. Thus, younger generations will have higher retirement ages, lower benefits and more exposure to individual private pensions. This is more or less a formula for creating intergenerational conflict, since it asks people in some specific cohorts to finance a state pension system at benefit levels that they will not experience. It is likely that any intergenerational polarization it creates is still less consequential than political identities shaped by other factors that are more deeply embedded in people's lives and in society. Health benefits are difficult to cut in this way because health care systems in most countries are relatively unified and hard to divide at any level (from high-level structures to the internal cross-subsidies within hospitals) but many of the policy techniques can also work in education, housing, and long-term care, with long-run bad results.

Equally, a focus on assembling coalitions in favour of win-win solutions changes the kinds of political thinking that is required. Consider, for example, the interaction of gender, work, and care. Gender inequalities are present in every policy conversation, but especially every conversation to do with ageing because women are disproportionately responsible for paid and unpaid caring. Policy in the interests of women should take this into account, and also try to change it. Dependency ratios depend on female labour force participation as well as the size of cohorts. Unpaid caring labour, whether it is children caring for parents, grandparents caring for grandchildren, or something else, is disproportionately done by women. Paid caring labour is likewise feminized, and becomes more so in the areas of the labour market that are less prestigious, protected and paid, such as home health aides or much of the workforce in nursing homes. All of this means that organizations concerned with the situation of women in society have multiple interests in the definition of ageing, the ageing policy agenda and the policies adopted. It is possible to imagine narrowly class-based definitions of women's interests, in which the interest of well-off working women in having cheap child and elder care is prioritized, but it is also possible to imagine, and in some countries see, much more encompassing approaches that align the interests of working women (in support for their family and work roles), paid carers (in salary and good conditions) and older people (in good support). The class-based approach simply offloads duties from overburdened working women onto less well-off working women, but women's organizations could also opt for broader coalitions and policies that are more inclusive and sustainable and permit coalitions with unions (representing the paid carers), providers who see benefit in offering a better quality product, and representatives of immigrants, who often are the paid carers. In other words, there is immense scope and incentive for interest groups to adopt a broader and more enlightened approach in their own self-interest.

7.4 Getting to a Win-Win

Bringing together the themes in this book, we can phrase our thesis so far as: there is no really important question about the politics of health that is best answered by analysing the politics of ageing. Nor does it work to infer politics, let alone policies, from demographics: people do not have or feel that they have clear interests shaped by demography and policymaking is driven by supply rather than demand. Instead, the right focus for explaining policies is on the supply side: the coalitions of policymakers and interest groups that put particular issues and policy ideas on the agenda.

One step is policy ideas: what are the policies that are win-win, that successfully balance interests that are often occluded, such as the interests of the care workforce, and that are based on a realistic evaluation of important factors such as the role of older people in providing unpaid care? A focus on policy ideas includes a focus on policy debate, which often means once again arguing against facile generational arguments. Constantly trying to quash zombie ideas is frustrating work, but it is not clear why stopping will help. Ceasing to try to argue with zombie ideas merely sets them up to become the conventional wisdom.

One point to underline in thinking about the policies is that life-course analysis is often taken to mean a focus on the young: a point of view that can be caricatured as the idea that the optimal return on investment in a person is a few months before birth, with declining returns every day afterwards. Life-course approaches mean what the term says: approaches over the life-course, which can and should include effective assistance and interventions at all ages. Life ends only at death, and so should life-course interventions.

A second step is coalitional politics. What are some organized groups with an interest in positive-sum approaches to health policy, including policies relevant to ageing? It includes groups with a commitment, based on a formulated understanding of their interests, to a sustainable approach to ageing and social care. Organized groups can do two things that disorganized voters, focused on other issues, cannot: formulate and debate complex policy options, and identify longer-term sustainability threats and possibilities.

A number of these organized groups stand out from our analysis. One is providers of health care and social care, whose interests in being financed to make any adaptations can lead to an interest in a quality and well structured system. Another is the formal caring workforce, typically organized, if organized at all, by public sector unions. They likewise have an incentive to promote a fiscally sustainable, high quality model of care, and to undercut insider/outsider divides that unions in other sectors can often promote. The formal caring workforce, like the informal caring workforce, is predominantly female, and women are at the centre of any likely sustainable policy solution. Women's movements can opt for many different definitions of the problems that women face, and their internal politics are complex and filled with their own representational inequalities. That makes their decisions particularly interesting, and shows the importance of highlighting the gender dimensions of this issue, on the level of individuals as well as society. Such an understanding has changed politics to a surprising degree, for example in Japan (Schoppa, 2010). Policymakers themselves can be important members of coalitions; health ministry officials, for example, will often have awareness of good and plausible policy options and skills at promoting them in coalition. Finally, organizations representing the elderly, especially the better established, have an interest in solutions that reflect the unselfishness of many elderly voters (who can care about their society and children as much as anybody) and in policy solutions that will be fiscally and politically sustainable over time.

This is a message of optimism. Instead of deterministic theories that read inexorable conflict and policy change from demographics, we have a world of complex coalitions and debates about policy ideas and agendas. The supply of ideas can be shaped by small numbers of people with policy skills, and the development of coalitions is flexible and can always offer new opportunities and ideas. Policy ideas that move towards positive-sum relations between people and groups and away from simple constraint and comparison can be developed. Instead of trying to infer inevitable policy from demographic patterns, we can embrace the complexity of politics and the possibilities that it brings. Instead of assuming, or creating, a zero-sum struggle between the generations, we can get positive-sum life-course policies. Instead of a world of winners and losers, we can make win-win policies. But we need to get the politics right.

Bibliography

Aagaard-Hansen, J., Norris, S. A., Maindal, H. T., Hanson, M. and Fall, C. (2019). What are the public health implications of the life course perspective? *Global Health Action*, 12(1), 1603491. https://doi.org/10.1080/16549716.2019.1603491 (accessed 25 January 2020)

Abou-Chadi, T. and Wagner, M. (2020). Electoral fortunes of social democratic parties: do second dimension positions matter? *Journal of European Public Policy*, 27(2), 246–72. https://doi.org/10.1080/13501763.2019.1701532 (accessed 19 March 2020).

Airey, L. (2003). 'Nae as nice a scheme as it used to be': lay accounts of neighbourhood incivilities and well-being. *Health & Place*, 9(2), 129–37.

Akhter, N., Bambra, C., Mattheys, K., Warren, J. and Kasim, A. (2018). Inequalities in mental health and well-being in a time of austerity: follow-up findings from the Stockton-on-Tees cohort study. *SSM – Population Health*, 6, 75–84. https://doi.org/10.1016/j.ssmph.2018.08.004 (accessed 19 March 2020).

Albacete, G. G. (2014). *Young people's political participation in Western Europe: continuity or generational change?* Palgrave Macmillan.

Allen, A. M., Thomas, M. D., Michaels, E. K. et al. (2019). Racial discrimination, educational attainment, and biological dysregulation among midlife African American women. *Psychoneuroendocrinology*, 99, 225–35.

Anderson, K. M. (2019). Financialisation meets collectivisation: occupational pensions in Denmark, the Netherlands and Sweden. *Journal of European Public Policy*, 26(4), 617–36. https://doi.org/10.1080/13501763.2019.1574309 (accessed 7 February 2020).

Anderson, K. M. and Lynch, J. (2007). Reconsidering Seniority Bias: Aging, Internal Institutions, and Union Support for Pension Reform. *Comparative Politics*, 39(2), 189–208. https://www.jstor.org/stable/20434033 (accessed 12 November 2019).

Annandale, E. and Hunt, K. (2000). *Gender inequalities in health*. Open University Press.

Ansell, B. (2014). The Political Economy of Ownership: Housing Markets and the Welfare State. *American Political Science Review*, 108(2), 383–402. https://doi.org/DOI: 10.1017/S0003055414000045 (accessed 1 December 2019).

Anxo, D., Bosch, G. and Rubery, J. (2010). Shaping the life course: a European perspective. In D. Anxo, G. Bosch and J. Rubery, eds., *The Welfare State and Life Transitions: A European Perspective*. Edward Elgar Publishing, pp. 1–78.

Arias, E. (2011). United States life tables, 2007. *National Vital Statistics Reports: From the Centers for Disease Control and Prevention, National Center for Health Statistics, National Vital Statistics System*, 59(9), 1–60.

Armingeon, K. and Bonoli, G. (2007). *The Politics of Post-Industrial Welfare States: Adapting Post-War Social Policies to New Social Risks*. Routledge. https://books.google.com/books?id=sTi2SS8egosC (accessed 1 December 2019).

Avendano, M. and Kawachi, I. (2014). Why do Americans have shorter life expectancy and worse health than do people in other high-income countries? *Annual Review of Public Health*, 35, 307–25. https://doi .org/10.1146/annurev-publhealth-032013-182411 (accessed 7 February 2020).

Bambra, C. (2011). *Work, worklessness, and the political economy of health*. Oxford University Press.

Bambra, C. (2016). *Health Divides: Where You Live Can Kill You*, 1st edn. Policy Press.

Bambra, C, ed. (2019). *Health in hard times: austerity and health inequalities*. Policy Press.

Bambra, C., Barr, B. and Milne, E. (2014). North and South: addressing the English health divide. *Journal of Public Health*, 36(2), 183–6. https://doi .org/10.1093/pubmed/fdu029 (accessed 12 November 2019).

Bambra, C., Fox, D. and Scott-Samuel, A. (2005). Towards a politics of health. *Health Promotion International*, 20(2), 187–93. https://doi.org/10.1093/ heapro/dah608 (accessed 12 November 2019).

Bambra, C., Lynch, J., and Smith, K. (2021). *The Unequal Pandemic: COVID-19 and Health Inequalities*. Bristol University Press.

Bambra, C., Riordan, R., Ford, J. and Matthews, F. (2020). The COVID-19 pandemic and health inequalities. *Journal of Epidemiology and Community Health*, jech-2020-214401. https://doi.org/10.1136/jech-2020-214401 (accessed 10 June 2020).

Bangham, G., Gardiner, L., Rahman, F. et al. (2019). *AN INTERGENERATIONAL AUDIT FOR THE UK: 2019*. https://www .resolutionfoundation.org/app/uploads/2019/06/Intergenerational-audit-for-the-UK.pdf (accessed 12 March 2020).

Barcevicius, E. and Weishaupt, T. (2014). *Assessing the Open Method of Coordination: Institutional Design and National Influence of EU Social Policy Coordination*. Work and Welfare in Europe series. Palgrave MacMillan.

Barlow, P. (2018). Does trade liberalization reduce child mortality in low- and middle-income countries? A synthetic control analysis of 36 policy experiments, 1963–2005. *Social Science & Medicine*, 205, 107–15. https://doi.org/10.1016/j.socscimed.2018.04.001 (accessed 3 March 2020).

Barlow, P., McKee, M., Basu, S. and Stuckler, D. (2017a). Impact of the North American Free Trade Agreement on high-fructose corn syrup supply in Canada: a natural experiment using synthetic control methods. *Canadian Medical Association Journal*, 189(26), E881–7. https://doi.org/10.1503/cmaj.161152 (accessed 12 November 2019).

Barlow, P., McKee, M., Basu, S. and Stuckler, D. (2017b). The health impact of trade and investment agreements: a quantitative systematic review and network co-citation analysis. *Globalization and Health*, 13(1), 13. https://doi.org/10.1186/s12992-017-0240-x (accessed 17 July 2020).

Barnard, H. (2019, 30 March). End the benefit freeze to stop people being swept into poverty. Joseph Rowntree Foundation. https://www.jrf.org.uk/report/end-benefit-freeze-stop-people-being-swept-poverty (accessed 4 April 2020).

Barnish, M., Tørnes, M. and Nelson-Horne, B. (2018). How much evidence is there that political factors are related to population health outcomes? An internationally comparative systematic review. *BMJ Open*, 8(10). https://doi.org/10.1136/bmjopen-2017-020886 (accessed 21 April 2020).

Barr, B., Bambra, C. and Whitehead, M. (2014). The impact of NHS resource allocation policy on health inequalities in England 2001–11: longitudinal ecological study. *BMJ*, 348, g3231. https://doi.org/10.1136/bmj.g3231 (accessed 3 March 2020).

Barr, B., Higgerson, J. and Whitehead, M. (2017). Investigating the impact of the English health inequalities strategy: time trend analysis. *BMJ*, 358, j3310. https://doi.org/10.1136/bmj.j3310 (accessed 13 January 2020).

Barr, B., Taylor-Robinson, D., Stuckler, D. et al. (2016). 'First, do no harm': are disability assessments associated with adverse trends in mental health? A longitudinal ecological study. *Journal of Epidemiology and Community Health*, 70(4), 339–45. https://doi.org/10.1136/jech-2015-206209 (accessed 13 May 2020).

Bartley, M. (2016). *Health Inequality: an Introduction to Concepts, Theories and Methods*. 2nd edn. Cambridge, UK/Malden, MA, USA.

Beaulac, J., Kristjansson, E. and Cummins, S. (2009). A systematic review of food deserts, 1966–2007. *Preventing Chronic Disease*, 6(3), A105.

Beckfield, J. (2018). *Political Sociology and the People's Health*. Oxford.

Beckfield, J. and Bambra, C. (2016). Shorter lives in stingier states: social policy shortcomings help explain the US mortality disadvantage. *Social Science & Medicine*, 171, 30–8. https://doi.org/10.1016/j.socscimed.2016.10.017 (accessed 17 November 2019.

Beckfield, J. and Krieger, N. (2009). Epi + demos + cracy: linking political systems and priorities to the magnitude of health inequities – evidence, gaps, and a research agenda. *Epidemiologic Reviews*, 31, 152–77. https://doi.org/10.1093/epirev/mxp002 (accessed 7 April 2020).

Ben, J., Cormack, D., Harris, R. and Paradies, Y. (2017). Racism and health service utilisation: a systematic review and meta-analysis. *PLoS One*, 12(12), e0189900.

Ben-Shlomo, Y. and Kuh, D. (2002). A life course approach to chronic disease epidemiology: conceptual models, empirical challenges and interdisciplinary perspectives. *International Journal of Epidemiology*, 31(2), 285–93. https://doi.org/10.1093/ije/31.2.285 (accessed 15 June 2019).

Beramendi P. (2012). *The Political Geography of Inequality. Regions and Redistribution*. Cambridge University Press.

Beramendi, P. and Rueda, D. (2007). Social Democracy Constrained: Indirect Taxation in Industrialized Democracies. *British Journal of Political Science*, 37(4), 619–41. http://www.jstor.org/stable/4497315 (accessed 11 June 2019).

Beramendi, P., Häusermann, S., Kitschelt, H. and Kriesi, H. (2015). Introduction: the Politics of Advanced Capitalism. In P. Beramendi, S. Hausermann, H. Kitschelt and H. Kriesi, eds., *The Politics of Advanced Capitalism*. Cambridge, pp. 1–64. https://doi.org/10.1017/CBO9781316163245.002 (accessed 7 April 2020).

Besley, T. and Kudamatsu, M. (2006). Health and democracy. *American Economic Review*, 96(2), 313–18.

Bhatti, Y. and Hansen, K. M. (2012). The effect of generation and age on turnout to the European Parliament – How turnout will continue to decline in the future. *Special Symposium: Generational Differences in Electoral Behaviour*, 31(2), 262–72. https://doi.org/10.1016/j.electstud.2011.11.004 (accessed 19 June 2019).

Birnbaum, S., Ferrarini, T. and Nelson, K. (2017). *The Generational Welfare Contract: Justice, Institutions and Outcomes*. Edward Elgar Publishing.

Birnie, K., Cooper, R., Martin, R. M. et al. (2011). Childhood Socioeconomic Position and Objectively Measured Physical Capability Levels in Adulthood: a Systematic Review and Meta-Analysis. *PLoS One*, 6(1), e15564. https://doi.org/10.1371/journal.pone.0015564 (accessed 17 April 2020).

Blouin, C., Chopra, M. and van der Hoeven, R. (2009). Trade and social determinants of health. *The Lancet*, 373(9662), 502–7. https://doi.org/10.1016/S0140-6736(08)61777-8 (accessed 7 April 2020).

Blow, C. M. (2020). The Brother Killer. New York Times, 12 April 2020.

Bohle, D. and Seabrooke, L. (2020). From asset to patrimony: the re-emergence of the housing question. *West European Politics*, 43(2), 412–34. https://doi.org/10.1080/01402382.2019.1663630 (accessed 6 March 2020).

Bollyky, T. J., Templin, T., Cohen, M. et al. (2019). The relationships between democratic experience, adult health, and cause-specific mortality in 170 countries between 1980 and 2016: an observational analysis. *The Lancet*, 393(10181), 1628–40. https://doi.org/10.1016/S0140-6736(19)30235-1 (accessed 16 March 2020).

Bonoli, G. and Häusermann, S. (2009). Who wants what from the welfare state? *European Societies*, 11(2), 211–32. https://doi.org/10.1080/14616690801942116 (accessed 24 March 2020).

Bos, V., Kunst, A. E., Keij-Deerenberg, I. M., Garssen, J. and Mackenbach, J. P. (2004). Ethnic inequalities in age- and cause-specific mortality in The Netherlands. *International Journal of Epidemiology*, 33(5), 1112–19. https://doi.org/10.1093/ije/dyh189 (accessed 6 July 2020).

Bovenberg, A. L. (2007). The life-course perspective and social policies: an overview of the issues. *CESifo Economic Studies*, 54(4), 593–641. https://doi.org/10.1093/cesifo/ifn029 (accessed 1 July 2020).

Braveman, P. A. (2009). Health Disparities Beginning in Child. *Pediatrics*, 124(November). DOI: 10.1542/peds.2009-1100D (accessed 29 November 2019).

Braveman, P. A., Cubbin, C., Egerter, S., Williams, D. R. and Pamuk, E. (2010). Socioeconomic disparities in health in the United States: what the patterns tell us. *American Journal of Public Health*, 100(S1), S186–96.

Bristow, J. (2019). *Stop Mugging Grandma. The 'Generation Wars' and Why Boomer Blaming Won't Solve Anything.* Yale University Press.

Buchholz, T. (2016). The Real Threat of an Aging Population. https://time.com/4356425/aging-population/ (accessed 25 May 2020).

Buck, D. and Maguire, D. (2015). *Inequalities in Life Expectancy: Changes over Time and Implications for Policy.* The King's Fund.

Busemeyer, M. R., Goerres, A. and Weschle, S. (2008). Demands for redistributive policies in an era of demographic aging: the rival pressures from age and class in 15 OECD countries. Max Planck Institute for the Study of Societies. https://www.ssoar.info/ssoar/bitstream/handle/document/19705/ssoar-2008-busemeyer_et_al-demands_for_redistributive_policies_in.pdf?sequence=1&isAllowed=y&lnkname=ssoar-2008-busemeyer_et_al-demands_for_redistributive_policies_in.pdf (accessed 29 November 2019).

Busemeyer, M. R., Goerres, A. and Weschle, S. (2009). Attitudes towards redistributive spending in an era of demographic ageing: the rival pressures from age and income in 14 OECD countries. *Journal of European Social Policy*, 19(3), 195–212. https://doi.org/10.1177/0958928709104736 (accessed 9 September 2019).

Busemeyer, M. R., Garritzmann, J. L., Neimanns, E. and Nezi, R. (2018). Investing in education in Europe: evidence from a new survey of public opinion. *Journal of European Social Policy*, 28(1), 34–54. https://doi.org/10.1177/0958928717700562 (accessed 2 November 2019).

Bussolo, M., Koettl, J. and Sinnott, E. (2015). *Golden Aging: Prospects for Healthy, Active, and Prosperous Aging in Europe and Central Asia.* World Bank Group. https://doi.org/10.1596/978-1-4648-0353-6 (accessed 6 December 2019).

Campbell, A. L. and Lynch, J. (2000). Whose 'Gray Power'? Elderly Voters, Elderly Lobbies, and Welfare Reform in Italy and the United States. *Italian Politics and Society*, 53, 11–39.

Case, A. and Deaton, A. (2015). Rising morbidity and mortality in midlife among white non-Hispanic Americans in the 21st century. *Proceedings of the National Academy of Sciences*, 112(49), 15078–83.

Case, A. and Deaton, A. (2017). Mortality and morbidity in the 21st century. *Brookings Papers on Economic Activity*, Spring 2017, 397–476.

Casey, B. H. (2012). The implications of the economic crisis for pensions and pension policy in Europe. *Global Social Policy*, 12(3), 246–65. https://doi .org/10.1177/1468018112455633 (accessed 20 October 2019).

Catalan Agency for Health Quality and Assessment (AQuAS). (2020). Coronavirus SARS-Cov-2 interactive map. http://aquas.gencat.cat/ .content/IntegradorServeis/mapa_covid/atlas.html (accessed 22 April 2020).

Cattaneo, M. A. and Wolter, S. C. (2009). Are the elderly a threat to educational expenditures? *European Journal of Political Economy*, 25(2), 225–36. https://doi.org/10.1016/j.ejpoleco.2008.10.002 (accessed 29 November 2019).

Caughey, D., O'Grady, T. and Warshaw, C. (2019). Policy Ideology in European Mass Publics, 1981–2016. *American Political Science Review*, 113(3), 674–93. https://doi.org/10.1017/S0003055419000157 (accessed 4 October 2019).

Celis-Morales, C. A., Welsh, P., Lyall, D. M. et al. (2018). Associations of grip strength with cardiovascular, respiratory, and cancer outcomes and all cause mortality: prospective cohort study of half a million UK Biobank participants. *BMJ*, 361, k1651. https://doi.org/10.1136/bmj .k1651 (accessed 9 January 2020).

Centre for Ageing Better. (2020). Doddery but dear?: examining age-related stereotypes. Centre for Ageing Better.

Chaney, P. (2013). Electoral Competition, Issue Salience and Public Policy for Older People: the Case of the Westminster and Regional UK Elections 1945–2011. *The British Journal of Politics and International Relations*, 15(3), 456–75. https://doi.org/10.1111/j.1467-856X.2011.00488.x (accessed 19 March 2020).

Chang, E.-S., Kannoth, S., Levy, S. et al. (2020). Global reach of ageism on older persons' health: a systematic review. *PloS One*, 15(1), e0220857–e0220857. https://doi.org/10.1371/journal.pone.0220857 (accessed 17 June 2020).

Chen, J. T. and Krieger, N. (2020). *Revealing the unequal burden of COVID-19 by income, race/ethnicity, and household crowding: US county vs ZIP code analyses.* https://cdn1.sph.harvard.edu/wp-content/uploads/sites/1266/2020/04/HCPDS_Volume-19_No_1_20_covid19_RevealingUnequalBurden_HCPDSWorkingPaper_04212020-1.pdf (accessed 7 July 2020).

Cheng, T. L. and Solomon, B. S. (2014). Translating Life Course Theory to clinical practice to address health disparities. *Maternal and Child Health Journal*, 18(2), 389–95. https://doi.org/10.1007/s10995-013-1279-9 (accessed 21 June 2020).

Cheng, T. L., Johnson, S. B. and Goodman, E. (2016). Breaking the intergenerational cycle of disadvantage: the three generation approach. *Pediatrics*, 137(6). https://doi.org/10.1542/peds.2015-2467 (accessed 17 December 2019).

Chiarini, B. (1999). The Composition of Union Membership: the Role of Pensioners in Italy. *British Journal of Industrial Relations*, 37(4), 577–600. https://doi.org/10.1111/1467-8543.00143 (accessed 5 November 2019).

CHRODIS. (n.d.). *The Welfare Watch Iceland.* http://chrodis.eu/wp-content/uploads/2017/03/the-welfare-watch.pdf (accessed 17 March 2020).

City of Chicago. (2020). *Public Health Healthy Chicago.* Chicago.Gov.

Clements, D. (2018). Caring for the elderly in an ageist society. *Spiked.* https://www.spiked-online.com/2018/11/05/caring-for-the-elderly-in-an-ageist-society/ (accessed 23 February 2020).

Colombo, F., Llena-Nozal, A., Mercier, J. and Tjadens, F. (2011). *Help Wanted?* OECD. https://doi.org/10.1787/9789264097759-en

Cooper, M. (2021). A burden on future generations? How we learned to hate deficits and blame the baby boomers. *The Sociological Review.* https://doi.org/10.1177/0038026121999211

Cooper, R. S., Wolf-Maier, K., Luke, A. et al. (2005). An international comparative study of blood pressure in populations of European vs. African descent. *BMC Medicine*, 3(1), 2.

Cummins, S., Curtis, S., Diez-Roux, A. V. and Macintyre, S. (2007). Understanding and representing 'place' in health research: a relational approach. *Social Science & Medicine*, 65(9), 1825–38.

Curtis, W. (2020, 21 May). The Striking Racial Divide in How Covid-19 Has Hit Nursing Homes. LAIST.

Cylus, J., Normand, C. and Figueras, J. (2019). *Will population ageing spell the end of the welfare state?: A review of evidence and policy options.* European Observatory on Health Systems and Policies.

Daykin, N. and Jones, M. (2008). Sociology and health. *Health Studies: An Introduction*, 108–46.

Doyal, L. (1995). *What Makes Women Sick: Gender and the Political Economy of Health*. Palgrave MacMillan.

Eggleston, J. and Munk, R. (2019). 'Net Worth of Households: 2015'. *Current Population Reports*. Washington D.C.

Esping-Andersen, G. (1990). *The Three Worlds of Welfare Capitalism*. Princeton University Press. https://doi.org/10.2307/2073705

European Social Survey Round 9. (2018, 1 November). NSD – Norwegian Centre for Research Data, Norway - Data archive and distributor of ESS data for ESS ERIC. https://www.europeansocialsurvey.org/data/ (accessed 9 April 2020).

Eurostat. (2020). Unemployment statistics.

EU-SILC. (2015). *EUROPEAN UNION STATISTICS ON INCOME AND LIVING CONDITIONS (EU-SILC)*. Eurostat.

Evans, R. G., McGrail, K. M., Morgan, S. G., Barer, M. L. and Hertzman, C. (2001). APOCALYPSE NO: Population Aging and the Future of Health Care Systems. *Canadian Journal on Aging/La Revue Canadienne Du Vieillissement*, 20(S1), 160–91. https://doi.org/DOI: 10.1017/S0714980800015282 (accessed 16 June 2020).

Fairlie, H. (1988). Talkin' 'Bout My Generation. *The New Republic*, 19–22.

Ferguson, N. and de Weck, J. (2019, June 5). European Millennials Are Not Like Their American Counterparts. *The Atlantic*. https://www.theatlantic.com/ideas/archive/2019/09/europes-young-not-so-woke/598783/ (accessed 5 July 2020).

Fernández, J. J. and Jaime-Castillo, A. M. (2013). Positive or negative policy feedbacks? Explaining popular attitudes towards pragmatic pension policy reforms. *European Sociological Review*, 29(4), 803–15. https://doi.org/10.1093/esr/jcs059 (accessed 13 September 2019).

Fleckenstein, T. (2011). The politics of ideas in welfare state transformation: Christian Democracy and the reform of family policy in Germany. *Social Politics*, 18(4), 543–71. https://doi.org/10.1093/sp/jxr022 (accessed 11 September 2020).

Forster, T., Kentikelenis, A. and Bambra, C. (2018). *Health Inequalities in Europe: Setting the Stage for Progressive Policy Action*. Dublin, Ireland.

Fowler, A. (2015). Regular Voters, Marginal Voters and the Electoral Effects of Turnout. *Political Science Research and Methods*, 3(2), 205–19. https://doi.org/10.1017/psrm.2015.18 (accessed 27 January 2020).

Freudenberg, N. (2016). *Lethal But Legal: Corporations, Consumption, and Protecting Public Health*. reprint edn. Oxford University Press.

Fuller, G. W., Johnston, A. and Regan, A. (2020). Housing prices and wealth inequality in Western Europe. *West European Politics*, 43(2),

297–320. https://doi.org/10.1080/01402382.2018.1561054 (accessed 30 June 2020).

Gallup Organisation. (2009). *Intergenerational solidarity.* Eurobarometer. http://ec.europa.eu/commfrontoffice/publicopinion/flash/fl_269_en.pdf (accessed 7 April 2020).

Garritzmann, J. L., Busemeyer, M. R. and Neimanns, E. (2018). Public demand for social investment: new supporting coalitions for welfare state reform in Western Europe? *Journal of European Public Policy,* 25(6), 844–61. https://doi.org/10.1080/13501763.2017.1401107 (accessed 17 March 2020).

Geys, B. (2006). Explaining voter turnout: a review of aggregate-level research. *Electoral Studies,* 25(4), 637–63. https://doi.org/10.1016/j .electstud.2005.09.002 (accessed 9 September 2019).

Giaimo, S. (2002). *Markets and Medicine: the Politics of Health Care Reform in Britain, Germany, and the United States.* University of Michigan Press. http://ebookcentral.proquest.com/lib/upenn-ebooks/detail .action?docID=3414551 (accessed 23 October 2019).

Gilens, M. (2012). *Affluence and Influence: Economic Inequality and Political Power in America.* Princeton University Press.

Gilleard, C. and Higgs, P. (2009). The Power of Silver: Age and Identity Politics in the 21st Century. *Journal of Aging & Social Policy,* 21(3), 277–95. https://doi.org/10.1080/08959420902955917 (accessed 17 March 2020).

Gingrich, J. and Ansell, B. W. (2015). The Dynamics of Social Investment: Human Capital, Activation, and Care. In P. Beramendi, S. Hausermann, H. Kitschelt and H. Kriesi, eds., *The Politics of Advanced Capitalism.* Cambridge University Press, pp. 282–304. https://doi.org/DOI: 10.1017/ CBO9781316163245.012 (accessed 19 October 2019).

Gjonca, A., Brockmann, H. and Maier, H. (2000). Old-Age Mortality in Germany prior to and after Reunification. *Demographic Research,* 3(1). https://doi.org/10.4054/DemRes.2000.3.1 (accessed 18 April 2020).

Gkiouleka, A., Huijts, T., Beckfield, J. and Bambra, C. (2018). Understanding the micro and macro politics of health: Inequalities, intersectionality and institutions – a research agenda. *Social Science & Medicine* (1982), 200, 92–8. https://doi.org/10.1016/j.socscimed.2018.01.025 (accessed 16 September 2019).

Goerres, A. (2007). Why are older people more likely to vote? The impact of ageing on electoral turnout in Europe. *The British Journal of Politics and International Relations,* 9(1), 90–121. https://doi.org/10.1111/j.1467-856x.2006.00243.x (accessed 31 January 2020).

Goerres, A. (2008). Reforming the Welfare State in Times of Grey Majorities: the Myth of an Opposition between Younger and Older Voters in Germany.

German Policy Studies, 1–21. https://papers.ssrn.com/abstract=1077604 (accessed 3 April 2020).

Goerres, A. (2009). *The Political Participation of Older People in Europe: the Greying of our Democracies*. Vol. 81. Palgrave Macmillan. https://doi .org/10.1057/9780230233959 (accessed 1 June 2020).

Goerres, A. and Tepe, M. (2010). Age-based self-interest, intergenerational solidarity and the welfare state: a comparative analysis of older people's attitudes towards public childcare in 12 OECD countries. *European Journal of Political Research*, 49(6), 818–51. https://doi.org/10.1111/ j.1475-6765.2010.01920.x (accessed 31 January 2020).

Goerres, A. and Vanhuysse, P. (2012). Mapping the Field: comparative Generational Politics and Policies in Ageing Democracies. In P. Vanhuysse and A. Goerres, eds., *Ageing Populations in Post-Industrial Democracies: Comparative Studies of Policies and Politics*. Routledge. https://books .google.com/books?hl=en&lr=&id=EVNB8B2bZIUC&oi=fnd&pg= PA1&dq=pensioner+parties&ots=a40FZkbIRC&sig=XmpYhxtr5DJ Axvd79YIHiIyunZI#v=onepage&q=pensioner parties&f=false (accessed 24 October 2019).

Gokhale, J., Raffelhüschen, B. and Walliser, J. (1994). The Burden of German Unification: a Generational Accounting Approach. *Working Papers* (WP 94-12). https://www.clevelandfed.org/newsroom-and-events/publications/ working-papers/working-papers-archives/1994-working-papers/wp-9412- the-burden-of-german-unification--a-generational-accounting-approach (accessed 11 March 2020).

Greer, S. L. (2015). John W. Kingdon, Agendas, Alternatives, and Public Policies. In M. Lodge, E. C. Page and S. J. Balla, eds., *The Oxford Handbook of Classics in Public Policy and Administration*. Oxford University Press, pp. 417–32). https://doi.org/10.1093/oxfordhb/9780199646135.013.18 (accessed 19 April 2020).

Greer, S. L. (2018). Labour politics as public health: how the politics of industrial relations and workplace regulation affect health, *European Journal of Public Health*, 28, 34–7. https://doi.org/10.1093/eurpub/cky163 (accessed 14 May 2020).

Greer, S. L. (2019). Comparative Federalism. As If Policy Mattered. 289-309 in S. L. Greer and H. Elliott, eds. *Federalism and Social Policy: Patterns of Redistribution in 11 Democracies*. University of Michigan Press.

Greer, S. L., Bekker, M. P. M., Azzopardi-Muscat, N. and McKee, M. (2018). Political analysis in public health: middle-range concepts to make sense of the politics of health. European Journal of Public Health, 28(Supp3), 3–6. https://doi.org/10.1093/eurpub/cky159 (accessed 1 May 2020).

Greer, S. L., Fahy, N., Rozenblum, S., Jarman, H., Palm, W., Elliott, H. A., and Wismar, M. (2019). *Everything you always wanted to know about*

European Union health policies but were afraid to ask. Revised second edition. Brussels: European Observatory on Health Systems and Policies.

Greer, S. L., King, E. J., da Fonseca, E. M., and Peralta-Santos, A. (2020). The comparative politics of COVID-19: The need to understand government responses. *Global public health*, 15(9), 1413–1416.

Greer, S.L., King, E.J., Peralta-Santos, A., and Massard da Fonseca, E. eds., (2021). *Coronavirus Politics: The Comparative Politics and Policy of COVID-19*. University of Michigan Press Open Access. https://www.press .umich.edu/11927713/coronavirus_politics

Gregoraci, G., van Lenthe, F. J., Artnik, B. et al. (2017). Contribution of smoking to socioeconomic inequalities in mortality: a study of 14 European countries, 1990–2004. *Tobacco Control*, 26(3), 260–8. https://doi.org/10.1136/tobaccocontrol-2015-052766 (accessed 1 July 2020).

Gustafsson, P. E., San Sebastian, M., Janlert, U. et al. (2014). Life-course accumulation of neighborhood disadvantage and allostatic load: empirical integration of three social determinants of health frameworks. *American Journal of Public Health*, 104(5), 904–10. https://doi.org/10.2105/ AJPH.2013.301707 (accessed 15 October 2019).

Hacker, J. S. (2004). Privatizing Risk without Privatizing the Welfare State: the Hidden Politics of Social Policy Retrenchment in the United States. *The American Political Science Review*, 98(2), 243–60. http://www.jstor .org/stable/4145310 (accessed 31 January 2020).

Hacker, J. S. and Pierson, P. (2014). After the 'master theory': Downs, Schattschneider, and the rebirth of policy-focused analysis. *Perspectives on Politics*, 12(03), 643–62.

Hall, P. A. and Soskice, D. (2001). *Varieties of Capitalism: the Institutional Foundations of Comparative Advantage*. Oxford University Press.

Hanley, S. (2010). The Emergence of Pensioners' Parties in Contemporary Europe. In J. C. Tremmel, ed., *A Young Generation Under Pressure?: The Financial Situation and the 'Rush Hour' of the Cohorts 1970–1985 in a Generational Comparison*. Springer-Verlag, pp. 225–47. http://doi .org/10.1007/978-3-642-03483-1_12 (accessed 2 May 2020).

Hanley, S. (2013). Explaining the success of pensioners' parties: a qualitative comparative analysis of 31 polities. In P. Vanhuysse and A. Goerres, eds., *Ageing Populations in Post-Industrial Democracies: Comparative Studies of Policies and Politics*. 1st edn. Routledge, pp. 23–53. https://www.taylorfrancis.com/books/e/9780203357415/ chapters/10.4324/9780203357415-8 (accessed 12 February 2020).

Häusermann, S. (2010). *The Politics of Welfare State Reform in Continental Europe: Modernization in Hard Times*. Cambridge University Press.

Hawe, P. and Shiell, A. (2000). Social capital and health promotion: a review. *Social Science & Medicine*, 51(6), 871–85.

Hay, D. (2019, 30 March). Change Universal Credit to help prevent homelessness. Joseph Rowntree Foundation. https://www.jrf.org.uk/blog/change-universal-credit-help-prevent-homelessness (accessed 2 May 2020).

Hemerijck, A. (2013). *Changing Welfare States*. Oxford University Press.

Hemerijck, A. (2017). *The Uses of Social Investment*. Oxford University Press.

Herd, P. and Moynihan, D. P. (2019). *Administrative Burden: Policymaking by Other Means*. Russell Sage Foundation.

Hill, K. Q. and Leighley, J. E. (1992). The Policy Consequences of Class Bias in State Electorates. *American Journal of Political Science*, 36(2), 351–65. https://doi.org/10.2307/2111481 (accessed 6 October 2019).

Hill, S. (2016). Axes of health inequalities and intersectionality. In K. E. Smith, C. Bambra and S. E. Hill, eds., *Health Inequalities: Critical Perspectives*. Oxford University Press, 95–108.

Hills, J. (2014). *Good Times, Bad Times: The Welfare Myth of Them and Us*. Policy Press.

Hills, J., De Agostini, P. and Sutherland, H. (2016). Benefits, pensions, tax credits and direct taxes. In *Social Policy in a Cold Climate: Policies and Their Consequences Since the Crisis*. EUROMOD, p. 11.

Hollingsworth, A., Ruhm, C. J. and Simon, K. (2017). Macroeconomic conditions and opioid abuse. *Journal of Health Economics*, 56, 222–33.

Holzer, H. and Sawhill, I. (2013, 23 April). Payments to elders are harming our future. *Washington Post*. https://www.washingtonpost.com/opinions/payments-to-elders-are-harming-our-future/2013/03/08/08c9030c-82bd-11e2-b99e-6baf4ebe42df_story.html (accessed 23 August 2019).

Homan, P. (2019). Structural Sexism and Health in the United States: a New Perspective on Health Inequality and the Gender System. *American Sociological Review*, 84(3), 486–516. https://doi.org/10.1177/0003122419848723 (accessed 2 May 2020).

Horn, B. P., Maclean, J. C. and Strain, M. R. (2017). Do Minimum Wage Increases Influence Worker Health? *Economic Inquiry*, 55(4), 1986–2007. https://doi.org/10.1111/ecin.12453 (accessed 12 June 2020).

Howe, N. and Strauss, W. (1992). *Generations: the History of America's Future, 1584 to 2069*. HarperCollins.

Howe, N. and Strauss, W. (2009). *Millennials Rising: the Next Great Generation*. Knopf Doubleday Publishing Group.

Hu, Y., van Lenthe, F. J., Judge, K. et al. (2016). Did the English strategy reduce inequalities in health? A difference-in-difference analysis comparing England with three other European countries. *BMC Public Health*, 16(1). https://doi.org/10.1186/s12889-016-3505-z (accessed 19 October 2019).

Huber, E. and Stephens, J. D. (2015). Postindustrial Social Policy. In P. Beramendi, S. Hausermann, H. Kitschelt and H. Kriesi, eds., *The Politics of Advanced Capitalism*. Cambridge University Press, pp. 259–81. https://doi.org/DOI: 10.1017/CBO9781316163245.011 (accessed 2 May 2020).

Huijts, T., Stornes, P., Eikemo, T. A. and Bambra, C. (2017). The social and behavioural determinants of health in Europe: findings from the European Social Survey (2014) special module on the social determinants of health. *European Journal of Public Health*, 27(Suppl1), 55–62. https://doi.org/10.1093/eurpub/ckw231 (accessed 7 March 2020).

ICNARC. (2020). Report on COVID-19 in critical care, 17 April 2020. Intensive Care National Audit and Research Centre.

IMF. (2004). *World Economic Outlook September 2004: the Global Demographic Transition. World economic outlook: a survey by the staff of the International Monetary Fund*. International Monetary Fund.

Immergut, E. M. and Anderson, K. M. (2009). Editors' Introduction: the Dynamics of Pension Politics. In E. M. Immergut, K. M. Anderson and I. Schulze, eds., *The Handbook of West European Pension Politics*. Oxford University Press, pp. 1–44. https://global.oup.com/academic/product/the-handbook-of-west-european-pension-politics-9780199562473?cc=it&lang=en& (accessed 2 May 2020).

Iversen, T. and Soskice, D. (2019). *Democracy and Prosperity: Reinventing Capitalism through a Turbulent Century*. Princeton University Press.

Jacobs, A. M. (2011). *Governing for the Long Term: Democracy and the Politics of Investment*. Cambridge University Press. https://doi.org/DOI: 10.1017/CBO9780511921766 (accessed 22 May 2020).

Jacobs, L. R. and Shapiro, R. Y. (2000). *Politicians Don't Pander: Political Manipulation and the Loss of Democratic Responsiveness*. University of Chicago Press.

Jarman, H. (2019). Normalizing Tobacco? The Politics of Trade, Investment, and Tobacco Control. *The Milbank Quarterly*, 97(2), 449–479.

Jarman, H., & Greer, S.L. (2010). Crossborder trade in health services: lessons from the European laboratory. *Health Policy*, 94(2), 158–163.

Jayawardana, S., Cylus, J. and Mossialos, E. (2019). It's not ageing, stupid: why population ageing won't bankrupt health systems. *European Heart Journal – Quality of Care and Clinical Outcomes*, 5(3), 195–201. https://doi.org/10.1093/ehjqcco/qcz022 (accessed 17 October 2019).

Jenson, J. and Saint-Martin, D. (2003). New Routes to Social Cohesion? Citizenship and the Social Investment State. *The Canadian Journal of Sociology/Cahiers Canadiens de Sociologie*, 28(1), 77–99. https://doi.org/10.2307/3341876 (accessed 22 May 2020).

Jerolmack, C. and Khan, S. (2014). Talk is cheap: ethnography and the attitudinal fallacy. *Sociological Methods & Research*, 43(2), 178–209.

Jitendra, A., Thorogood, E. and Hadfield-Spoor, M. (2018). *Left behind: is Universal Credit truly Universal?* The Trussell Trust, Salisbury.

Jones, N. L., Gilman, S. E., Cheng, T. L. et al. (2019). Life Course Approaches to the Causes of Health Disparities. *American Journal of Public Health*, 109(S1), S48–55. https://doi.org/10.2105/AJPH.2018.304738 (accessed 22 May 2020).

Kalache, A. and Kickbusch, I. (1997). A global strategy for healthy ageing. *World Health*, 50(4), 4–5.

Keen, R., Kennedy, S. and Wilson, W. (2017). Universal Credit roll-out: Autumn/Winter 2017. https://researchbriefings.parliament.uk/ResearchBriefing/Summary/CBP-8096 (accessed 15 December 2019).

Key, V. O. and Heard, A. (1949). *Southern Politics in State and Nation*. Alfred A. Knopf.

Kibele, E. U. B., Klüsener, S. and Scholz, R. D. (2015). Regional Mortality Disparities in Germany. *KZfSS Kölner Zeitschrift Für Soziologie Und Sozialpsychologie*, 67(1), 241–70. https://doi.org/10.1007/s11577-015-0329-2 (accessed 7 December 2019).

Kingdon, J. W. (2010). *Agendas, Alternatives, and Public Policies*. Pearson.

Kissau, K., Lutz, G. and Rosset, J. (2012). Unequal Representation of Age Groups In Switzerland. *Representation*, 48(1), 63–81. https://doi.org/10.1080/00344893.2012.653241 (accessed 22 May 2020).

Kohli, M. (1999). Private and public transfers between generations: linking the family and the state. *European Societies*, 1(1), 81–104. https://doi.org/10.1080/14616696.1999.10749926 (accessed 5 September 2019).

Kohli, M. (2015). Generations in Aging Societies: Inequalities, Cleavages, Conflicts. In C. Torp, ed., *Challenges of Aging: Pensions, Retirement and Generational Justice*. Palgrave Macmillan, pp. 265–88. https://doi.org/10.1057/9781137283177_14 (accessed 25 October 2019).

Koivusalo, M. (2014). Policy space for health and trade and investment agreements. *Health Promotion International*, 29(Suppl1), i29–47. https://doi.org/10.1093/heapro/dau033 (accessed 9 November 2019).

Komp, K. (2013). Political Gerontology: Population Ageing and the State of the State. In K. Komp and M. Aartsen, eds., *Old Age In Europe: a Textbook of Gerontology*. Springer, pp. 59–77. https://doi.org/10.1007/978-94-007-6134-6_5 (accessed 15 January 2020).

Komp, K. and van Tilburg, T. (2010). Ageing societies and the welfare state: where the inter-generational contract is not breached. *International Journal of Ageing and Later Life*, 5(1), 7–11. https://doi.org/10.3384/ijal.1652-8670.10517 (accessed 1 July 2020).

Konzelmann, L., Wagner, C. and Rattinger, H. (2012). Turnout in Germany in the course of time: life cycle and cohort effects on electoral turnout from

1953 to 2049. *Electoral Studies*, 31(2), 250–61. https://doi.org/10.1016/j
.electstud.2011.11.006 (accessed 11 September 2020).

Kramer, M. R. and Hogue, C. R. (2009). Is segregation bad for your health?
Epidemiologic Reviews, 31(1), 178–94.

Krieger, N. (2001). Theories for social epidemiology in the 21st century:
an ecosocial perspective. *International Journal of Epidemiology*, 30(4),
668–77. https://doi.org/10.1093/ije/30.4.668 (accessed 17 June 2020).

Krieger, N., Chen, J. T., Coull, B., Waterman, P. D. and Beckfield, J. (2013).
The unique impact of abolition of Jim Crow laws on reducing inequities
in infant death rates and implications for choice of comparison groups
in analyzing societal determinants of health. *American Journal of Public
Health*, 103(12), 2234–44. https://doi.org/10.2105/AJPH.2013.301350
(accessed 19 April 2020).

Krieger, N., Kosheleva, A., Waterman, P. D. et al. (2014). 50-year trends in US
socioeconomic inequalities in health: US-born Black and White Americans,
1959–2008. *International Journal of Epidemiology*, 43(4), 1294–313.
https://doi.org/10.1093/ije/dyu047 (accessed 6 May 2020).

Krieger, T. and Ruhose, J. (2013). Honey, I shrunk the kids' benefits – revisiting
intergenerational conflict in OECD countries. *Public Choice*, 157(1),
115–43. https://doi.org/10.1007/s11127-013-0064-z (accessed 1 July 2020).

Krugman, P. (1991). Increasing Returns and Economic Geography. *Journal
of Political Economy*, 99(3), 483–99. https://doi.org/10.1086/261763
(accessed 16 October 2019).

Kudamatsu, M. (2012). Has Democratization Reduced Infant Mortality in
Sub-Saharan Africa? Evidence from Micro Data. *Journal of the European
Economic Association*, 10(6), 1294–317. https://doi.org/10.1111/j.1542-
4774.2012.01092.x (accessed 14 July 2020).

Kuh, D., Karunananthan, S., Bergman, H. and Cooper, R. (2014). A life-course
approach to healthy ageing: maintaining physical capability. *Proceedings
of the Nutrition Society*, 73(2), 237–48. https://doi.org/10.1017/
S0029665113003923 (accessed 21 June 2020).

Kuh, D., Ben-Shlomo, Y., Lynch, J., Hallqvist, J. and Power, C. (2003).
Life course epidemiology. *Journal of Epidemiology and Community
Health*, 57(10), 778–83. http://www.ncbi.nlm.nih.gov/entrez/query.
fcgi?cmd=Retrieve&db=PubMed&dopt=Citation&list_uids=14573579
(accessed 4 May 2020).

Lambelet, A. (2011). Understanding the Political Preferences of Seniors'
Organizations. The Swiss Case. *Swiss Political Science Review*, 17(4),
417–31. https://doi.org/10.1111/j.1662-6370.2011.02036.x (accessed
12 October 2019).

Laurence, J. (2002). Why an ageing population is the greatest threat to society.
The Independent, 10 April 2002.

Lenhart, O. (2017). Do Higher Minimum Wages Benefit Health? Evidence from the UK. *Journal of Policy Analysis and Management*, 36(4), 828–52. https://doi.org/10.1002/pam.22006 (accessed 25 October 2019).

Levy, J. (1999). Vice into Virtue? Progressive Politics and Welfare Reform in Continental Europe. *Politics & Society*, 27(2), 239–73. https://doi.org/10.1177/0032329299027002004 (accessed 12 December 2019).

Lieberman, T. (2013, 14 March). The enduring myth of the Greedy Geezer. *Columbia Journalism Review*. http://www.cjr.org/united_states_project/the_enduring_myth_of_the_greed.php (accessed 22 October 2019).

Lijphart, A. (1997). Unequal Participation: Democracy's Unresolved Dilemma. *American Political Science Review*, 91(1), 1–14. https://doi.org/10.2307/2952255 (accessed 2 September 2019).

Lindvall, J. and Rueda, D. (2014). The Insider–Outsider Dilemma. *British Journal of Political Science*, 44(2), 460–75. https://doi.org/DOI: 10.1017/S0007123412000804 (accessed 4 August 2019).

Link, B. G. and Phelan, J. (1995). Social conditions as fundamental causes of disease. *Journal of Health and Social Behavior*, Extra issue, 80–94.

Litt, J. S., Tran, N. L. and Burke, T. A. (2002). Examining urban brownfields through the public health 'macroscope'. *Environmental Health Perspectives*, 110(Suppl2), 183–93.

Loopstra, R., Reeves, A. and Stuckler, D. (2015). Rising food insecurity in Europe. *The Lancet*, 385(9982), 2041. https://doi.org/10.1016/S0140-6736(15)60983-7 (accessed 29 July 2019).

Loopstra, R., Fledderjohann, J., Reeves, A. and Stuckler, D. (2018). Impact of Welfare Benefit Sanctioning on Food Insecurity: a Dynamic Cross-Area Study of Food Bank Usage in the UK. *Journal of Social Policy*, 47(3), 437–57. https://doi.org/10.1017/S0047279417000915 (accessed 24 September 2019).

Loopstra, R., Reeves, A., McKee, M. and Stuckler, D. (2015). Do punitive approaches to unemployment benefit recipients increase welfare exit and employment? A cross-area analysis of UK sanctioning reforms. *Sociology Working Papers, Oxford University* (2015–01).

Lundberg, O. (2008). Commentary: Politics and public health – some conceptual considerations concerning welfare state characteristics and public health outcomes. *International Journal of Epidemiology*, 37(5), 1105–8. https://doi.org/10.1093/ije/dyn078 (accessed 12 December 2019).

Lynch, J. (2001). The Age-Orientation of Social Policy Regimes in OECD Countries. *Journal of Social Policy*, 30(3), 411–36. http://search.proquest.com/docview/61521790?pq-origsite=summon (accessed 30 October 2019).

Lynch, J. (2006). *Age in the Welfare State: the Origins of Social Spending on Pensioners, Workers, and Children.* Cambridge University Press. https://doi.org/10.1017/CBO9780511606922 (accessed 5 December 2019).

Lynch, J. (2020). *Regimes of Inequality: the Political Economy of Health and Wealth.* Cambridge University Press. https://books.google.com/books?id=d4K0DwAAQBAJ (accessed 5 July 2020).

Lynch, J. and Myrskylä, M. (2009). Always the Third Rail? Pension Income and Policy Preferences in European Democracies. *Comparative Political Studies,* 42(8), 1068–97. https://doi.org/10.1177/0010414009331722 (accessed 11 June 2020).

Maas, J., Verheij, R. A., Groenewegen, P. P., Vries, de S. and Spreeuwenberg, P. (2006). Green space, urbanity, and health: how strong is the relation? *Journal of Epidemiology & Community Health,* 60(7), 587–92. https://doi.org/10.1136/jech.2005.043125 (accessed 22 July 2020).

McClean, C. T. (2019). *Does It Matter That Politicians Are Older Than Their Constituents? Yes.* https://cpb-us-e1.wpmucdn.com/sites.dartmouth.edu/dist/d/274/files/2019/09/McClean-2019.pdf (accessed 29 May 2020).

McEwen, B. S. and Stellar, E. (1993). Stress and the individual: mechanisms leading to disease. *Archives of Internal Medicine,* 153(18), 2093–101.

Macintyre, S. (2007). Deprivation amplification revisited; or, is it always true that poorer places have poorer access to resources for healthy diets and physical activity? *International Journal of Behavioral Nutrition and Physical Activity,* 4(1), 32.

Macintyre, S., Ellaway, A. and Cummins, S. (2002). Place effects on health: how can we conceptualise, operationalise and measure them? *Social Science & Medicine,* 55(1), 125–39.

McNamara, C. L., Balaj, M., Thomson, K. H., Eikemo, T. A. and Bambra, C. (2017). The contribution of housing and neighbourhood conditions to educational inequalities in non-communicable diseases in Europe: findings from the European Social Survey (2014) special module on the social determinants of health. *European Journal of Public Health,* 27(Suppl1), 102–6. https://doi.org/10.1093/eurpub/ckw224 (accessed 30 July 2019).

Mackenbach, J. P. (2010). Has the English strategy to reduce health inequalities failed? *Social Science & Medicine,* 71(7), 1249–53. https://doi.org/10.1016/j.socscimed.2010.07.014 (accessed 4 November 2019).

Mackenbach, J. P. (2012). The persistence of health inequalities in modern welfare states: the explanation of a paradox. *Social Science & Medicine,* 75(4), 761–9. https://doi.org/10.1016/j.socscimed.2012.02.031 (accessed 4 November 2019).

Mackenbach, J. P. (2017). Nordic paradox, Southern miracle, Eastern disaster: persistence of inequalities in mortality in Europe. *European Journal of*

Public Health, 27(Suppl4), 14–17. https://doi.org/10.1093/eurpub/ckx160 (accessed 5 May 2020).

Mackenbach, J. P., Kulhánová, I., Artnik, B. et al. (2016). Changes in mortality inequalities over two decades: register based study of European countries. *BMJ*, 353, i1732. https://doi.org/10.1136/bmj.i1732 (accessed 2 April 2020).

Madureira Lima, J. and Galea, S. (2018). Corporate practices and health: a framework and mechanisms. *Globalization and Health*, 14, 21. https://doi.org/10.1186/s12992-018-0336-y (accessed 5 November 2019).

Maeder, P. (2015). *THE LIFE-COURSE PERSPECTIVE IN SOCIAL POLICY*. https://www.lives-nccr.ch/en/newsletter/life-course-perspective-social-policy-n1673 (accessed 21 November 2019).

Mair, P. (2013). *Ruling the void: the hollowing of western democracy*. Verso.

Markowitz, G. and Rosner, D. (2003). *Deceit and Denial: The Deadly Politics of Industrial Pollution*. University of California Press.

Marmot, M. (2004, 7 June). *Status syndrome: how your social standing directly affects your health and life expectancy*. University College London.

Marmot, M. (2015). *The Health Gap: The Challenge of an Unequal World*. 1st edn. Bloomsbury.

Marmot, M., Friel, S., Bell, R., Houweling, T. A. and Taylor, S. (2008). Closing the gap in a generation: health equity through action on the social determinants of health. *The Lancet*, 372(9650), 1661–9. https://doi.org/10.1016/S0140-6736(08)61690-6 (accessed 28 October 2019).

Marron, D. (2017). Smoke gets in your eyes: what is sociological about cigarettes? *Sociological Review*, 65(4), 882–97. https://doi.org/10.1111/1467-954X.12404 (accessed 8 August 2019).

Mello, L. de, Schotte, S., Tiongson, E. R. and Winkler, H. (2017). Greying the Budget: Ageing and Preferences over Public Policies. *Kyklos*, 70(1), 70–96. https://doi.org/10.1111/kykl.12131 (accessed 2 December 2019).

Melo, D. F. and Stockemer, D. (2014). Age and political participation in Germany, France and the UK: a comparative analysis. *Comparative European Politics*, 12(1), 33–53. https://doi.org/10.1057/cep.2012.31 (accessed 18 September 2019).

Mertens, D. (2017). The 'New Welfare State' under Fiscal Strain. In A. Hemerijck, ed., *The Uses of Social Investment*. Oxford Scholarship.

Molla, M. T. (2013). Expected years of life free of chronic condition-induced activity limitations – United States, 1999–2008. *CDC Health Disparities and Inequalities Report – United States*, 62(3), 87.

Morel, N., Palier, B. and Palme, J., eds. (2012). *Towards a social investment welfare state?* 1st edn. Bristol University Press. https://doi.org/10.2307/j.ctt9qgqfg (accessed 28 May 2020).

Morgan, K. J. (2002). Forging the Frontiers Between State, Church, and Family: Religious Cleavages and the Origins of Early Childhood Education and Care Policies in France, Sweden, and Germany. *Politics & Society*, 30(1), 113–48. https://doi.org/10.1177/0032329202030001005 (accessed 28 March 2020).

Morgan, K. J. (2013). Path Shifting of the Welfare State: Electoral Competition and the Expansion of Work–Family Policies in Western Europe. *World Politics*, 65(1), 73–115. https://doi.org/DOI: 10.1017/S0043887112000251 (accessed 9 April 2020).

Mosley, L. (2000). Room to move: international financial markets and national welfare states. *International Organization*, 54(4), 737–73. https://web.stanford.edu/class/polisci243b/readings/v0002068.pdf (accessed 11 January 2020).

Naczyk, M. (2013). Agents of privatization? Business groups and the rise of pension funds in Continental Europe. *Socio-Economic Review*, 11(3), 441–69. https://doi.org/10.1093/ser/mws012 (accessed 8 November 2019).

NAO. (2016). *Benefit sanctions*. National Audit Office.

National Academies of Sciences, Engineering, and Medicine (2021). *High and Rising Mortality Rates Among Working-Age Adults* (K. M. Harris, M. Majmundar and T. Becker, eds.) Washington, DC. The National Academies Press. doi:10.17226/25976

National Research Council and Institute of Medicine (2013). *U.S. Health in International Perspective: Shorter Lives, Poorer Health*. (S. H. Woolf and L. Aron, eds.) National Academies Press. https://doi.org/10.17226/13497 (accessed 10 September 2019).

National Transfer Accounts. (2012). Understanding the Generational Economy. https://ntaccounts.org/web/nta/download-confirm (accessed 24 June 2020).

Naumann, E. (2014). Increasing conflict in times of retrenchment? Attitudes towards healthcare provision in Europe between 1996 and 2002. *International Journal of Social Welfare*, 23(3), 276–86. https://doi.org/10.1111/ijsw.12067 (accessed 10 December 2019).

Navarro, V. (2019). Why the White Working-class Mortality and Morbidity is Increasing in the United States: the Importance of the Political Context. *International Journal of Health Services: Planning, Administration, Evaluation*, 49(2), 197–203. https://doi.org/10.1177/0020731419832236 (accessed 2 February 2020).

Nazroo, J. Y. and Williams, D. R. (2006). The social determination of ethnic/racial inequalities in health. *Social Determinants of Health*, 2, 238–66.

Nolte, E. and McKee, M. (2011). Variations in amenable mortality – trends in 16 high-income nations. *Health Policy*, 103(1), 47–52. https://doi.org/10.1016/j.healthpol.2011.08.002 (accessed 21 April 2020).

Nolte, E., Scholz, R., Shkolnikov, V. and McKee, M. (2002). The contribution of medical care to changing life expectancy in Germany and Poland. *Social Science & Medicine*, 55(11), 1905–21. https://doi.org/10.1016/s0277-9536(01)00320-3 (accessed 9 December 2019).

OECD. (2017). *Pensions at a Glance 2017: OECD and G20 Indicators*. OECD Publishing.

ONS. (2018). Health Profile for England 2018. Chapter 5: inequalities in health. Office for National Statistics. https://www.gov.uk/government/publications/health-profile-for-england-2018/chapter-5-inequalities-in-health (accessed 21 December 2019).

ONS. (2019). Health state life expectancies by national deprivation deciles, England and Wales. Office for National Statistics. https://www.ons.gov.uk/peoplepopulationandcommunity/healthandsocialcare/healthinequalities/bulletins/healthstatelifeexpectanciesbyindexofmultipledeprivationimd/2015to2017?hootPostID=e68fa582ca53a887a9117570ec1f5e82 (accessed 12 February 2020).

ONS. (2020). Deaths involving COVID-19 by local area and socioeconomic deprivation: deaths occurring between 1 March and 17 April 2020. Office for National Statistics.

Otjes, S. and Krouwel, A. (2018). Old Voters on New Dimensions: Why Do Voters Vote for Pensioners' Parties? The Case of the Netherlands. *Journal of Aging & Social Policy*, 30(1), 24–47. https://doi.org/10.1080/08959420.2017.1363589 (accessed 7 September 2019).

Ottersen, O. P., Dasgupta, J., Blouin, C. et al. (2014). The political origins of health inequity: prospects for change. *The Lancet*, 383(9917), 630–67. https://doi.org/10.1016/S0140-6736(13)62407-1 (accessed 29 October 2019).

Owen, A. L. and Wu, S. (2007). Is Trade Good for Your Health? *Review of International Economics*, 15(4), 660–82.

Pampel, F. C. and Williamson, J. B. (1989). *Age, class, politics, and the welfare state*. Cambridge University Press. https://franklin.library.upenn.edu/catalog/FRANKLIN_9911655683503681 (accessed 21 April 2020).

Pearce, J. (2013). Commentary: financial crisis, austerity policies, and geographical inequalities in health. *Environment and Planning A: Economy and Space*, 45(9), 2030–45. https://doi.org/10.1068/a4663 (accessed 17 February 2020).

Pearce, J. R., Richardson, E. A., Mitchell, R. J. and Shortt, N. K. (2010). Environmental justice and health: the implications of the socio-spatial distribution of multiple environmental deprivation for health inequalities in the United Kingdom. *Transactions of the Institute of British Geographers*, 35(4), 522–39.

Perera, I. (2018). States of Mind: a Comparative and Historical Study on the Political Economy of Mental Health. *Publicly Accessible Penn Dissertations*.

https://repository.upenn.edu/edissertations/3172 (accessed 2 December 2019).

Perera, I. M. (2019). Mental health and politics since the eurozone crisis: the role of mental health professionals. *European Psychiatry*, 62, 28–9. https://doi.org/10.1016/j.eurpsy.2019.08.014 (accessed 15 May 2020).

Pettinger, T. (2019). The impact of an ageing population on the economy. Economics Help. https://www.economicshelp.org/blog/8950/society/impact-ageing-population-economy/ (accessed 25 May 2020).

Pevalin, D. J., Reeves, A., Baker, E. and Bentley, R. (2017). The impact of persistent poor housing conditions on mental health: a longitudinal population-based study. *Preventive Medicine*, 105, 304–10. https://doi.org/10.1016/j.ypmed.2017.09.020 (accessed 2 September 2019).

Phelan, J. C., Link, B. G. and Tehranifar, P. (2010). Social Conditions as Fundamental Causes of Health Inequalities: Theory, Evidence, and Policy Implications. *Journal of Health and Social Behavior*, 51(1Suppl), S28–40. https://doi.org/10.1177/0022146510383498 (accessed 20 August 2019).

Phelan, J. C., Link, B. G., Diez-Roux, A., Kawachi, I. and Levin, B. (2004). 'Fundamental causes' of social inequalities in mortality: a test of the theory. *Journal of Health and Social Behavior*, 45(3), 265–85.

Pickett, K. and Wilkinson, R. (2010). *The Spirit Level: Why Equality is Better for Everyone*. New edn. Penguin.

Pickett, K. E. and Wilkinson, R. G. (2015). Income inequality and health: a causal review. *Social Science & Medicine*, 128, 316–26. https://doi.org/10.1016/j.socscimed.2014.12.031 (accessed 16 January 2020).

Pierson, P. (1994). *Dismantling the welfare state?: Reagan, Thatcher and the politics of retrenchment*. Cambridge University Press. https://books.google.it/books?hl=it&lr=&id=0eoHZjR7Sw8C&oi=fnd&pg=PR7&dq=pierson+1994+&ots=aYMkNwZdrJ&sig=VQfdMRlG3OG2sg04t9L8zPBaisI#v=onepage&q=pierson 1994&f=false (accessed 25 April 2020).

Pierson, P. (1996). The New Politics of the Welfare State. *World Politics*, 48(2), 143–79. https://doi.org/DOI: 10.1353/wp.1996.0004 (accessed 23 September 2019).

Pontusson, J. and Rueda, D. (2010). The Politics of Inequality: Voter Mobilization and Left Parties in Advanced Industrial States. *Comparative Political Studies*, 43(6), 675–705.

populationpyramid.net. (2019). Population Pyramids of the World from 1950 to 2100. https://www.populationpyramid.net/lithuania/2020/ (accessed 2 June 2020).

PHE. (2018). *A review of recent trends in mortality in England*. Public Health England.

Putnam, R. (1993). The prosperous community: social capital and public life. *American Prospect*, 13(Spring), Vol. 4. http://www. prospect. org/print/vol/13 (accessed 7 April 2003).

Quiggin, J. (2010). *Zombie Economics: How dead ideas still walk among us.* Princeton University Press.

Rajan, S., Cylus, J., and McKee, M. (2020). What do countries need to do to implement effective 'find, test, trace, isolate and support' systems? *Journal of the Royal Society of Medicine,* 113(7), 245–250.

Rechel, B., Jagger, C. and McKee, M. (2020). *Living Longer, but in Better or Worse Health?* European Observatory on Health Systems and Policies.

Reeves, A. (2017a). Commentary: uncertainties in addressing the 'health gap'. *International Journal of Epidemiology,* 46(4), 1324–8. https://doi.org/10.1093/ije/dyx183 (accessed 3 December 2019).

Reeves, A. (2017b). Does sanctioning disabled claimants of unemployment insurance increase labour market inactivity? An analysis of 346 British local authorities between 2009 and 2014. *Journal of Poverty and Social Justice,* 25(2), 129–46. https://doi.org/10.1332/175982717X14939739331029 (accessed 19 December 2019).

Reeves, A., McKee, M. and Stuckler, D. (2015). The attack on Universal Health Coverage in Europe: recession, austerity, and unmet needs. *European Journal of Public Health,* 25(3), 364–5.

Reeves, A., Clair, A., McKee, M. and Stuckler, D. (2016). Reductions in the United Kingdom's Government Housing Benefit and Symptoms of Depression in Low-Income Households. *American Journal of Epidemiology,* 184(6), 421–9. https://doi.org/10.1093/aje/kww055 (accessed 6 January 2020).

Reeves, A., McKee, M., Mackenbach, J., Whitehead, M. and Stuckler, D. (2017a). Introduction of a National Minimum Wage Reduced Depressive Symptoms in Low-Wage Workers: a Quasi-Natural Experiment in the UK. *Health Economics,* 26(5), 639–55. https://doi.org/10.1002/hec.3336 (accessed 26 June 2020).

Reeves, A., McKee, M., Mackenbach, J., Whitehead, M. and Stuckler, D. (2017b). Public pensions and unmet medical need among older people: cross-national analysis of 16 European countries, 2004–2010. *Journal of Epidemiology and Community Health,* 71(2), 174–80. https://doi.org/10.1136/jech-2015-206257 (accessed 9 September 2019).

Richardson, H. (2019). In-work poverty hits 2.9 million children. BBC News Article, 30 March 2019. https://www.bbc.com/news/education-47734733 (accessed 23 July 2020).

Robinson, T., Brown, H., Norman, P. D. et al. (2019). The impact of New Labour's English health inequalities strategy on geographical inequalities in infant mortality: a time-trend analysis. *Journal of Epidemiology and Community Health,* 73(6), 564–8. https://doi.org/10.1136/jech-2018-211679 (accessed 14 May 2020).

Rodrik, D. (2012). *The Globalization Paradox.* Oxford University Press.

Roser, M., Ortiz-Ospina, E. and Ritchie, H. (2019). *Life Expectancy*. Published online at OurWorldinData.org. https://ourworldindata.org/life-expectancy (accessed 10 March 2020).

Rueda, D. (2015). The State of the Welfare State: Unemployment, Labor Market Policy, and Inequality in the Age of Workfare. *Comparative Politics*, 47(3), 296–314. http://www.jstor.org/stable/43664148 (accessed 8 November 2019).

Ruhm, C. J. (2018). *Deaths of despair or drug problems?* NBER Working Paper No. 24188.

Sabbagh, C. and Vanhuysse, P. (2010). Intergenerational Justice Perceptions and the Role of Welfare Regimes: a Comparative Analysis of University Students. *Administration & Society*, 42(6), 638–67. https://doi.org/10.1177/0095399710377440 (accessed 17 August 2019).

Safire, W. (2007). *Third Rail*. New York Times Magazine.

Sammons, P., Hall, J., Smees, R. et al. (2015). *Evaluation of children's centres in England (ECCE). Strand 4: The impact of children's centres: studying the effects of children's centres in promoting better outcomes for young children and their families.* https://ore.exeter.ac.uk/repository/handle/10871/23328 (accessed 11 October 2019).

Sanz, I. and Velázquez, F. J. (2007). The role of ageing in the growth of government and social welfare spending in the OECD. *European Journal of Political Economy*, 23(4), 917–31. https://doi.org/10.1016/j.ejpoleco.2007.01.003 (accessed 6 January 2020).

Scheve, K. and Stasavage, D. (2016). *Taxing the Rich: a History of Fiscal Fairness in the United States and Europe*. Princeton University Press.

Schminke, T. (2019, 10 November). How different generations voted in the EU election. *Europe Elects*. https://europeelects.eu/2019/06/03/how-different-generations-voted-in-the-eu-election/ (accessed 25 April 2020).

Schoppa, L. (2010). Exit, voice, and family policy in Japan: limited changes despite broad recognition of the declining fertility problem. *Journal of European Social Policy*, 20(5), 422–32. https://doi.org/10.1177/0958928710380477 (accessed 1 October 2019).

Schoppa, L. J. (2006). *Race for the Exits*. 1st edn. Cornell University Press. http://www.jstor.org/stable/10.7591/j.ctt7zjsw (accessed 27 September 2019).

Schram, A., Labonte, R., Baker, P. et al. (2015). The role of trade and investment liberalization in the sugar-sweetened carbonated beverages market: a natural experiment contrasting Vietnam and the Philippines. *Globalization and Health*, 11, 41. https://doi.org/10.1186/s12992-015-0127-7 (accessed 9 November 2019).

Schrecker, T. (2017). Was Mackenbach right? Towards a practical political science of redistribution and health inequalities. *Health & Place*, 46,

293–99. https://doi.org/10.1016/j.healthplace.2017.06.007 (accessed 16 April 2020).

Schrecker, T. and Bambra, C. (2015). *How Politics Makes Us Sick: Neoliberal Epidemics*. Palgrave Macmillan.

Schultheis, E. (2018). Why young Germans are feeling gloomy about their country. BBC News article, 12 May 2018. http://www.bbc.com/capital/story/20180926-why-young-germans-are-feeling-gloomy-about-their-country (accessed 4 May 2020).

Schumacher, G., Vis, B. and van Kersbergen, K. (2013). Political parties' welfare image, electoral punishment and welfare state retrenchment. *Comparative European Politics*, 11(1), 1–21. https://doi.org/10.1057/cep.2012.5 (accessed 11 November 2020).

Scott-Samuel, A., Bambra, C., Collins, C. et al. (2014). The impact of Thatcherism on health and well-being in Britain. *International Journal of Health Services: Planning, Administration, Evaluation*, 44(1), 53–71. https://doi.org/10.2190/HS.44.1.d (accessed 17 November 2019).

Shapiro, T. M. (2017). *Toxic Inequality: How America's Wealth Gap Destroys Mobility, Deepens the Racial Divide, and Threatens Our Future*. Basic Books.

Shelton, C. A. (2008). The aging population and the size of the welfare state: Is there a puzzle? *Journal of Public Economics*, 92(3), 647–51. https://doi.org/10.1016/j.jpubeco.2007.10.002 (accessed 3 September 2019).

Skalická, V., van Lenthe, F., Bambra, C., Krokstad, S. and Mackenbach, J. (2009). Material, psychosocial, behavioural and biomedical factors in the explanation of relative socio-economic inequalities in mortality: evidence from the HUNT study. *International Journal of Epidemiology*, 38(5), 1272–84.

Smith, J. C. and Medalia, C. (2014). *Health Insurance Coverage in the United States: 2013*. NBER.

Smith, K. E. (2007). Health inequalities in Scotland and England: the contrasting journeys of ideas from research into policy. *Social Science & Medicine*, 64(7), 1438–49. https://www.sciencedirect.com/science/article/abs/pii/S0277953606005892 (accessed 28 November 2019).

Smith, K. E. (2013). *Beyond Evidence-Based Policy in Public Health*. Palgrave Macmillan.

Sonmez, F. (2020). Texas Lt. Gov. Dan Patrick comes under fire for saying seniors should 'take a chance' on their own lives for sake of grandchildren during coronavirus crisis. Washington Post, 24 March 2020.

Sørensen, R. J. (2013). Does aging affect preferences for welfare spending? A study of peoples' spending preferences in 22 countries, 1985–2006. *European Journal of Political Economy*, 29, 259–71. https://doi.org/10.1016/j.ejpoleco.2012.09.004 (accessed 12 December 2019).

Statista. (2020). Median age of the population in Spain from 1950 to 2050. https://www.statista.com/statistics/275398/median-age-of-the-population-in-spain/ (accessed 24 May 2020).

Streeck, W. and Mertens, D. (2013). Public Finance and the Decline of State Capacity in Democratic Capitalism. In A. Schäfer and W. Streeck, eds., *Politics in the Age of Austerity*. Policy Press, pp. 25–58.

Strully, K. W., Rehkopf, D. H. and Xuan, Z. M. (2010). Effects of Prenatal Poverty on Infant Health: State Earned Income Tax Credits and Birth Weight. *American Sociological Review*, 75(4), 534–62.

Superintendence of Public Health. (2012). *A Healthy Weight for Life: a National Strategy for Malta*. Superintendence of Public Health Ministry for Health, the Elderly and Community Care. Msida. https://deputyprimeminister. gov.mt/en/Documents/National-Health-Strategies/hwl_en.pdf (accessed 6 April 2020).

Taylor, A. (2011). Older Adult, Older Person, Senior, Elderly or Elder: a Few Thoughts on the Language we use to Reference Aging. British Columbia Law Institute. https://www.bcli.org/older-adult-older-person (accessed 24 May 2020).

Taylor-Robinson, D., Lai, E. T. C., Wickham, S. et al. (2019). Assessing the impact of rising child poverty on the unprecedented rise in infant mortality in England, 2000–2017: time trend analysis. *BMJ Open*, 9(10), e029424.

Tepe, M. and Vanhuysse, P. (2010). Elderly bias, new social risks and social spending: change and timing in eight programmes across four worlds of welfare, 1980–2003. *Journal of European Social Policy*, 20(3), 217–34. https://doi.org/10.1177/0958928710364436 (accessed 6 January 2020).

Thane, P. (2005). *A History of Old Age*. J. Paul Getty Museum.

Thelen, K. (2014). *Varieties of Liberalization and the New Politics of Social Solidarity. Cambridge Studies in Comparative Politics*. Cambridge University Press. https://doi.org/DOI: 10.1017/CBO9781107282001 (accessed 19 October 2019).

Thomson, D. W. (1989). The welfare state and generation conflict: winners and losers. In P. A. Johnson, C. Conrad and D. Thomson, eds., *Workers Versus Pensioners: Intergenerational Justice in an Ageing World*. Manchester University Press, pp. 35–56.

Thomson, D. W. (1993). A lifetime of privilege? Aging and generations at century's end. In V. L. Bengtson and W. A. Achenbaum, eds., *The Changing Contract Across Generations*. Hawthorne: Aldine de Gruyter, pp. 215–37.

Tiberj, V. (2017). *Les citoyens qui viennent: Comment le renouvellement générationnel transforme la politique en France [The citizens who are coming: how generational renewal is transforming politics in France]*. PUF.

Torres, J. M. and Waldinger, R. (2015). Civic stratification and the exclusion of undocumented immigrants from cross-border health care. *Journal of Health and Social Behavior*, 56(4), 438–59. https://doi.org/10.1177/0022146515610617 (accessed 29 March 2020).

Tosun, M. S., Williamson, C. R. and Yakovlev, P. (2012). Elderly Migration and Education Spending: Intergenerational Conflict Revisited. *Public Budgeting & Finance*, 32(2), 25–39. https://doi.org/10.1111/j.1540-5850.2012.01007.x (accessed 26 April 2020).

UN Department of Economic and Social Affairs. (2020). World Population Prospects 2019. https://population.un.org/wpp/DataQuery/ (accessed 24 May 2020).

Van de Velde, S., Huijts, T., Bracke, P. and Bambra, C. (2013). Macro-level gender equality and depression in men and women in Europe. *Sociology of Health and Illness*, 35(5), 682–98. https://doi.org/10.1111/j.1467-9566.2012.01521.x (accessed 21 August 2019).

Vidovičová, L. and Honelová, M. (2018). A Case Study of Ageism in Political Debates: are Social Media a Latent Source of Generational Hatred? *Slovensky Narodopis-Slovak Ethnology*, 66(2), 203–20. https://doi.org/10.26363/SN.2018.2.03 (accessed 22 January 2020).

Vincent, J. A. (2003). Demography, Politics and Old Age. In *British Society for Gerontology Annual Conference, Newcastle upon Tyne* (Vol. 15). http://people.exeter.ac.uk/JVincent/Conference papers/BSG Newcastle/Newcastle Paper.doc (accessed 15 October 2019).

Vlandas, T. (2017). Grey power and the Economy: Aging and Inflation across Advanced Economies. *Comparative Political Studies*, 51(4), 514–52. https://doi.org/10.1177/0010414017710261 (accessed 21 July 2019).

Volkens, A., Burst, T., Krause, W. et al. (2020). *Manifesto Project Dataset*. Manifesto Project (MRG/CMP/MARPOR). https://manifesto-project.wzb.eu/datasets (accessed 7 July 2020).

Walczak, A., van der Brug, W. and de Vries, C. E. (2012). Long- and short-term determinants of party preferences: Inter-generational differences in Western and East Central Europe. *Electoral Studies*, 31(2), 273–84. https://doi.org/10.1016/j.electstud.2011.11.007 (accessed 19 September 2019).

Walton, H., Dajnak, D., Beevers, S. et al. (2015). *Understanding the health impacts of air pollution in London*. Kings College London for Transport for London and the Greater London Authority, 1(1), 6–14.

Wang, J. and Caminada, K. (2017). *Leiden LIS budget incidence fiscal redistribution dataset on Income Inequality*. LIS Data Center.

Wang, Y., Mechkova, V. and Andersson, F. (2018). Does Democracy Enhance Health? New Empirical Evidence 1900–2012. *Political Research Quarterly*, 106591291879850. https://doi.org/10.1177/1065912918798506 (accessed 30 November 2019).

Weaver, R. K. and Torp, C. (2015). Policy Feedbacks and Pension Policy Change. In C. Torp, ed., *Challenges of Aging: Pensions, Retirement and Generational Justice* (pp. 61–82). Palgrave Macmillan. https://doi .org/10.1057/9781137283177_5 (accessed 1 August 2019).

Whitehead, M. (1991). The concepts and principles of equity and health. *Health Promotion International*, 6(3), 217–28. https://doi.org/10.1093/ heapro/6.3.217 (accessed 19 December 2019).

Whitehead, M. and Popay, J. (2010). Swimming upstream? Taking action on the social determinants of health inequalities. *Social Science & Medicine*, 71(7), 1234–6. https://doi.org/10.1016/j.socscimed.2010.07.004 (accessed 6 June 2020).

Whittaker, D. and Thorsteinsson, G. (2016). *The Iceland Watch: A land that thinks outwards and forwards*. Mereo Books.

WHO. (2003). *WHO Framework Convention on Tobacco Control*. World Health Organization.

WHO. (2007). *Women, Ageing and Health: a Framework for Action*. World Health Organization. http://whqlibdoc.who.int/publications/ 2007/9789241563529_eng.pdf (accessed 26 January 2020).

WHO. (2015). *The Minsk Declaration – The Life-course Approach in the Context of Health 2020. WHO European Ministerial Conference on the Life- course Approach in the Context of Health 2020*. World Health Organization. http://www.euro.who.int/__data/assets/pdf_file/0009/289962/The-Minsk- Declaration-EN-rev1.pdf?ua=1 (accessed 17 March 2020).

WHO. (2018). *The life-course approach: from theory to practice. Case stories from two small countries in Europe*. World Health Organization. http:// www.euro.who.int/__data/assets/pdf_file/0004/374359/life-course-iceland- malta-eng.pdf?ua=1 (accessed 22 June 2020).

Wigley, S. and Akkoyunlu-Wigley, A. (2011). Do electoral institutions have an impact on population health? *Public Choice*, 148(3–4), 595–610. https:// doi.org/10.1007/s11127-010-9686-6 (accessed 17 September 2019).

Wilensky, H. L. (1975). *The welfare state and equality: structural and ideological roots of public expenditures*. University of California Press. https://franklin.library.upenn.edu/catalog/FRANKLIN_991213613503681 (accessed 21 October 2019).

Williams, D. R., Lawrence, J. A. and Davis, B. A. (2019). Racism and Health: Evidence and Needed Research. *Annual Review of Public Health*, 40(1), null. https://doi.org/10.1146/annurev-publhealth-040218-043750 (accessed 25 March 2020).

Williams, G., Cylus, J., Roubal, T., Ong, P. and Barber, S. (2019). *Will population ageing lead to uncontrolled health expenditure growth?* European Observatory on Health Systems and Policies.

Winant, G. (2021). The Natural Profits of Their Years of Labor: Mass Production, Family, and the Politics of Old Age. *Radical History Review*, 2021(139), 75–102.

Wisensale, S. K. (2013). Austerity vs. solidarity: intergenerational conflict in the European Union. *International Journal of Humanities and Social Science*, 3(1), 21–30.

Wittenberg, R., Hu, B. and Hancock, R. (2018). *Projections of Demand and Expenditure on Adult Social Care 2015 to 2040*. London. https://www .pssru.ac.uk/publications/pub-5421/ (accessed 12 April 2020).

World Bank. (1994). *Averting the Old Age Crisis. A World Bank Policy Research Report*. https://doi.org/10.1007/BF02681086 (accessed 7 November 2019).

Zaninotto, P., Batty, G. D., Stenholm, S. et al. (2020). Socioeconomic Inequalities in Disability-free Life Expectancy in Older People from England and the United States: a Cross-national Population-Based Study. *The Journals of Gerontology: Series A*, 75(5), 906–13. https://doi.org/10.1093/ gerona/glz266 (accessed 6 July 2020).

Index